"In this truly pathbreaking research on school dropouts, Louie F. Rodríguez presents the reader with a theoretical framework that positions the concept of recognition—together with individual agency, opportunity, and power—at its center. Without apology, he challenges practitioners, educators, and school leaders to disavow the depersonalizing, power-evasive, and alienating impacts of most U.S. schooling today by incorporating a constructive, consciousness-building politics of recognition into their praxis. Kudos to Dr. Rodríguez for his invaluable contribution to an otherwise stalled articulation of school dropout in both scholarly and public policy debates."

> —*Angela Valenzuela, College of Education, University of Texas at Austin;*
> *Author of* Subtractive Schooling *and* Leaving Children Behind

"There is no more important issue in education than the lack of achievement and attainment of Black and Latina/o students along all segments of the educational pipeline. This empirical fact is an example of the failure of the U.S. education system to educate all of our youth. One could argue that the high school 'dropout' crisis is the segment of the pipeline where we lose the largest number of our students of color. In *The Time Is Now*, Louie F. Rodríguez provides convincing evidence from 10 years of research that the talent we lose when we fail to graduate our Black and Latina/o high school students is a devastating loss to the U.S. domestically and globally. The answers that Rodríguez provides are centered on the assets and strengths that exist with these students and their families—assets and strengths that are often ignored by the schools. Those who want to better understand this crisis and work to increase the numbers of students through high school and other segments of the educational pipeline must read the racial justice lessons of *The Time Is Now*."

> —*Daniel G. Solorzano, Professor of Social Science and Comparative Education,*
> *Graduate School of Education and Information Studies,*
> *University of California, Los Angeles*

"*The Time Is Now* provides much-needed insight on the critical need to significantly reduce the dropout crisis in the U.S. Simply stated, we can't educate students who are not in an education setting. Our human capital must be one of America's prize assets to progress as a country, democracy, and society in the twenty-first century. With each student we lose, it is a significant debit out of America's economic, social, and moral bank. *The Time Is Now* highlights the lost opportunities as well as those that still remain to rectify the breaches in the pipeline to provide all students an opportunity to learn. The book is not only informative and instructive, but serves as a compelling call to action and a reminder that the best time to address yesterday's mistakes and today's challenges is now."

> —*John H. Jackson, President and CEO, Schott Foundation for Public Education*

THE TIME IS NOW

Studies in the
Postmodern Theory of Education

Shirley R. Steinberg
General Editor

Vol. 457

The Counterpoints series is part of the Peter Lang Education list.
Every volume is peer reviewed and meets
the highest quality standards for content and production.

PETER LANG
New York • Washington, D.C./Baltimore • Bern
Frankfurt • Berlin • Brussels • Vienna • Oxford

LOUIE F. RODRÍGUEZ

THE **TIME** IS **NOW**

Understanding and Responding to the Black and Latina/o Dropout Crisis in the U.S.

PETER LANG
New York • Washington, D.C./Baltimore • Bern
Frankfurt • Berlin • Brussels • Vienna • Oxford

Library of Congress Cataloging-in-Publication Data

Rodríguez, Louie F.
The time is now: understanding and responding to the black and latina/o
dropout crisis in the U.S. / Louie F. Rodríguez.
pages cm. — (Counterpoints: studies in the postmodern theory of education; vol. 457)
Includes bibliographical references and index.
1. High school dropouts—United States—Prevention.
2. African Americans—Education (Secondary) 3. Hispanic Americans—
Education (Secondary) 4. African American high school students—Social conditions.
5. Hispanic American high school students—Social conditions. I. Title.
LC146.5.R63   373.12'913—dc23   2013032455
ISBN 978-1-4331-2374-0 (hardcover)
ISBN 978-1-4331-2373-3 (paperback)
ISBN 978-1-4539-1217-1 (e-book)
ISSN 1058-1634

Bibliographic information published by **Die Deutsche Nationalbibliothek**.
Die Deutsche Nationalbibliothek lists this publication in the "Deutsche
Nationalbibliografie"; detailed bibliographic data is available
on the Internet at http://dnb.d-nb.de/.

The paper in this book meets the guidelines for permanence and durability
of the Committee on Production Guidelines for Book Longevity
of the Council of Library Resources.

© 2014 Peter Lang Publishing, Inc., New York
29 Broadway, 18th floor, New York, NY 10006
www.peterlang.com

Printed in the United States of America

Table of Contents

List of Figures and Tables

Foreword

A recent report from the U.S. Department of Education announced that for the first time in many years, graduation rates are rising and dropout rates are declining. Based on the AFGR (Averaged Freshman Graduation Rate), the nation's 2009–2010 graduation rate was 78.2%. This was the highest rate recorded since 1974. Interestingly, few explanations were offered for the good news, aside from platitudes from public officials about the hard work of educators; as if prior to this year, they had been sleeping on the job. Nonetheless, the fact that more students are graduating is clearly good news, but does it mean that the dropout crisis is over? A closer look at the numbers reveals that 21.8% of students in 2009–2010 did not graduate. Further examination shows that in most major cities throughout the United States, as many as 50% of students drop out before graduation. The vast majority of these are Latino and African American males, the same groups that continue to fill our nation's prisons at an alarming rate.

Aside from considerable hand-wringing, most public officials offer very little in the way of a strategic plan for confronting the problem. U.S. Education Secretary, Arne Duncan, has asserted that he wants to shut down as many as 5,000 "dropout factories," yet he has not offered any explanation for why these schools are failing (including dozens in Chicago that operated under his leadership there as Chief Education Officer), nor has he spelled out where the students who attend these schools will be placed.

Numerous studies have shown that for students who do not graduate, the consequences can be disastrous. According to the Child Trends Data Bank (www.childtrends.org/databank/?q=mode/373) statistics on the full- and part-time employment rate in 2011 among young people between the ages of 16 to 24 who dropped out of high school, less than 50 percent were employed. In contrast, the employment rate for high-school graduates with no college attainment was 61%; for those with some college or an associate degree, 75%; and for those with a bachelor's degree or higher, 86%. The Alliance for Excellent Education (www.all4ed.org/about_the_crisis/impact) estimates "that if the 1.3 million high school dropouts from the Class of 2010 had earned their diplomas instead of dropping out, the U.S. economy would have seen an additional $337 billion in wages over these students' lifetimes." The costs to communities where poverty rates are highest are even more damaging. Intergenerational poverty is highly associated with school failure and low educational attainment.

There is no question that the nation is facing a crisis caused by the persistence of high dropout rates. The question is: why and for whom? Clearly, the nation has learned to live with high dropout rates for many years, and the poverty and unemployment that are associated with school failure have been part of the social landscape for a very long time.

Undoubtedly, part of the reason why this crisis has been tolerated is because high dropout rates have been rationalized as a by-product of laziness and a lack of motivation on the part of students. The widely held perception is that students who drop out leave school voluntarily. According to this view, they drop out to sleep late, get high, and hang out with friends. Not surprisingly, if people believe that those who drop out have chosen to do so because they are lazy, they are also more likely to conclude that dropouts have no one to blame but themselves.

A widely aired commercial featuring Miami Heat basketball star, LeBron James, vividly depicts how these assumptions are operationalized. The commercial shows a young man sleeping in bed, refusing to heed his mother's admonition to go to school because he would rather sleep. Suddenly, the young man drops through the bed and quickly descends into a homeless shelter. He wakes up startled, and then rushes off to school. LeBron is seen in the back of the classroom smiling approvingly at the choice the young man has made.

The message is powerful, but what if it were wrong? What if large numbers of students were not dropping out by choice, but because they faced obstacles that made attending school regularly difficult? What if they stop attending school because they have to work, care for siblings or sick relatives, or navigate dangerous streets? What if some are actually pushed out by school administrators who understand that one way to raise test scores is to remove students who bring down the mean? What if some stop attending simply because school is too boring and they see no purpose in what they are required to learn?

In *The Time Is Now: Understanding and Responding to the Black and Latina/o Dropout Crisis in the United States*, Louie Rodriguez draws on ten years of research carried out in urban schools across the United States to explore the factors influencing the dropout phenomenon. Readers will learn that rather than a matter of laziness, dropping out is a complex process that occurs over time, and is highly influenced by the character and culture of schools. In this insightful study, readers will also learn what might be done to prevent and reduce the likelihood that students will drop out of school.

To educators, parents, and policy makers this book will be an invaluable resource for responding to the dropout crisis. Rather than offering slogans, platitudes, or simplistic solutions, Rodriguez goes deep within schools to understand why relationships with teachers are often weak or strained. He also shows us, by drawing on the voices of students, that this is a problem that can be solved. Given the costs of continued failure, this book could not have come along at a better time.

Pedro A. Noguera
New York City
February 9, 2013

Preface

Supreme Court Justice nominee and Harvard Law Professor, Lani Guinier, coauthored a book with Gerald Torres in 2002 titled, *The Miner's Canary*. Guinier and Torres (2002) used the miner's canary as a metaphor to explain the condition of race in the United States. They went on to describe how miners use canaries to alert them of the toxicity of the air in the mine. The toxicity in the air causes considerable distress to the canary's overly sensitive respiratory system, and thus becomes a signal to the miners that they must vacate the mine. The canary's condition, as a result of the toxic environment, suggests that something is wrong, that the miners are in danger, and that they will die if nothing is done. Unfortunately, in the case of the miner's canary, the canary dies.

Guinier and Torres believe that race in society functions like the miner's canary. Through racial marginalization, Guinier and Torres argued that people of color have been signaling to the rest of society that something is wrong, that they are in danger, and that they will remain in danger if nothing is done. They went on to propose an alternative way to discuss, analyze, and act for racial justice so that society is more responsive and politically just in the way it interacts with people of color in the United States.

Analogous to the miner's canary, my work over the last 10 years has encouraged a similar analysis of the canary in society. However, rather than focusing on society in general, I have been interested in understanding and responding to the dropout crisis through the lived experiences and perspectives of mostly low-income *Black* and *Latina/o* students in U.S. schools. In my analysis of the student experience in Boston, Miami, and Southern California, the canary has become our Black and Latina/o youth who drop out at rates of 50% or higher. And the 21st-century mine is the classroom. My school-based research has shown that the air in some of our schools is toxic for many of our youth. The toxicity is evident by high dropout rates, low college-going rates, the school-to-prison pipeline, school environments that produce physical and symbolic violence, individual feelings of disconnectedness from school, community contexts of political and economic despair, and ongoing questions about the purpose and relevance of school. When Black and Latina/o students do succeed, it is largely because they are able to find those "pockets of hope" (de los Reyes & Gozemba, 2001) in schools that nurture their personal, emotional, and academic selves.

In reference to students in this book, I am deliberately referring to Black and Latina/o students, because these are the two groups of students I worked with across the three regions. I deliberately use the term Black, because many of my students were not, nor did they consider themselves, African American. In Boston, I worked with Cape Verdean, Jamaican, and African American students; and in Miami, I worked with a significant Haitian population. Many students would tell me, "hey mister, I'm not African American, I'm Black." I was also sensitive to the direct and indirect political influence that the Black Power Movement may have had on the self-ascribed labels students chose to identify with racially and ethnically. In other words, "Black" is an all-encompassing descriptor that captures African-Diaspora groups that were present in all three cities where I worked—Boston, Miami, and Southern California. The Latina/o label is somewhat similar. In Boston, I worked with Dominican and Puerto Rican students (or "Spanish kids"), and low-income Cuban students in Miami. In Southern California, I worked with *Chicana/o*, Latina/o, and Central American students. Interestingly, many of the Latina/o students I worked with in California were curious about the Chicana/o label, as they were at least one generation removed from the Chicana/o Movement, and some students were first-generation students whose parents did not live through the Movement. Nonetheless, the students were interested.

Nonetheless, in response to the toxic air in our schools and classrooms, the so-called reformers and reform efforts tend to focus on redesigning the mine itself. They question the size of the mine. They focus on the color of the mine. They focus on the number of canaries in the mine. Some even blame the miner and canary for not being able to succeed in this often toxic environment. The walls of the mine could be caving in, but the miner and the canary are largely expected to succeed without any attention placed on the conditions and toxicity of the environment within the mine. There is hardly any attention on the air itself, what produces the air, where might there be clear and healthy air pockets in the mine; and there is a far less likelihood of anyone ever asking the miner or the canary what is going on, what is wrong, and what can be done to possibly improve the situation.

In my research across three demographically similar regions of the United States, low-income students of color often feel silenced, yet have plenty to say. They also yearn for connectedness and meaning in school. They thirst for quality relationships with their peers and adults (Valenzuela, 1999). Our students want to teach *and* learn. They want to engage in meaningful learning experiences that actually matter to their lives and their communities. And our students want to inspire those that come after them, and to be inspired by the people who came before them. Yet, some of the conditions that currently exist in school are far more likely to "export" students who express dissent (Fine, 1991), or graduate others with very little purpose or consciousness about who they are in their communities and society, and yet some of our students do graduate, are college ready, and make a relatively successful transition to college. This is certainly the case where I have conducted my research and where most of our children are likely to attend school—large, urban centers that house enormous high schools, sometimes filled with unprepared teachers; hampered by inadequate learning resources; and surrounded by social, economic, and political conditions that often stagnate equitable opportunities to learn (Noguera, 2003).

In recognition of the many challenges facing low-income schools and communities, there is considerable research on the challenges facing low-income Black and Latina/o youth. This is not a book that aims to replicate those efforts. Rather, this book aims to offer some perspective on the education of Black and Latina/o youth by providing a series of insights and suggestions from my work over the last 10 years in these communities. In the context of our schools and classrooms, and extending the metaphor of Guinier and Torres's (2002) miner's canary, I ask, Who is singing? Who stopped singing? Why? What can we learn from our students? What about quiet students, or those silenced by policies, practices, and processes in school? What about the students who are not engaged with school, not involved in activities, and not taking the most selective classes? What about the students who are critical of school, who get in trouble, or who are on the verge of dropping out or transferring to a continuation school? How can our canaries help us understand the environment so we can create healthy environments where all can thrive? I am particularly concerned with Black and Latina/o youth, because my work confirms what years of empirical research continues to tell us—our system continues to struggle to impartially and adequately engage these students in a dignified, equitable, and socially just manner. While there are examples of success all over the country, by and large, these two groups continue to receive a less than adequate education in the richest country in the world.

In this book, I argue that the ways in which dropout has been studied and understood are partially the reason why this crisis is persistent and concentrated in communities of color (Valencia, 2011). I also propose a progressive framework that urges stakeholders to take a complex look at the problem, not just for the sake of analysis, but for the sake of action. I discuss why school culture may very well be the missing link in the research that aims to respond to the dropout crisis, as it provides vital perspective on what is wrong, what is right, and what can be done in our nation's public schools so that more students will not stop singing or all together perish by falling into the abyss of downward mobility. I then offer a series of research-based recommendations that bridge school- and community-based action, and I close by providing some lessons learned that may inform the work of local communities in responding to the dropout crisis.

Why Dropout?

In 1998 I left my home, affectionately known as the "IE" (Inland Empire—Inland region of Southern California), to begin graduate school at Harvard University. At Harvard I studied under the umbrella program of Administration, Planning and Social Policy with a concentration in Communities and Schools. I was mentored by some of the country's leading scholars in education, including Pedro Noguera, Richard Elmore, Eleanor Drago-Severson, Mark Warren, and Gilberto Conchas. As Pedro Noguera's lead research assistant on a major research project across several Boston-area high schools, I soon began to carve out a research study that evolved into my dissertation. I was particularly intrigued by the student experience, namely of Black and Latina/o youth, in urban high schools. This was an incredible opportunity to work with an expansive research team that valued student voice and prioritized the perspectives and experiences of historically marginalized youth; and to be surrounded by a mentor and research team who believed in the principle of "reciprocity" in educational research. That is, not only would we be collecting data and conducting research, but we were committed to serving the schools and communities we were involved with by recommending and shaping policies and practices with relevant stakeholders across the schools.

The ethnographic, phenomenological, and case-study methodology that I eventually designed for my dissertation was shaped by the everyday experiences I had while engaging with the local schools and communities. For two years, I spent countless hours observing youth in classrooms, hallways, at lunchtime, before and after school; and I walked to and from school with many of the students I shadowed. I took copious field notes and commanded the skill of interviewing. In this work, I discovered the complex task of straddling the roles of researcher and advocate for youth, many of whom often sought me out for mentorship, along with members of the research team, as several of us were able to connect with the students economically, culturally, and politically.

In addition to my dissertation research, I also made my way into schools and communities during my doctoral studies, first as a middle-school counselor and program coordinator, and then as an elementary and high school teacher. Steeped deeply in the principles of Critical Pedagogy, and rooted in the lived experiences of the historically marginalized populations of the

Northeast, I began to engage in a series of reflections and connections about and between the literature to which I became so intimately connected, the lives of the people I served and learned from in the local community, and later, my own experiences as a working-class Chicano who attended public schools in Southern California. As I witnessed Freire's notion of domesticated schooling emerge for the teachers and students in the local schools, I began to see how this concept, in retrospect, painted my own K–12 experiences when I lived in Southern California. I also began to reflect upon those liberatory moments that I experienced, and began to wonder why they had not been more common. When I began to take a historical look at educational inequality in the United States, analyze the political nature of educational policy and policymaking, and delve deeply into the roots of social inequality, I realized that my domesticated educational experiences were not accidental, but were, in fact, by design.

A formative moment during graduate school came during my first year in a course called Politics and Policy-Making taught by Richard Elmore (who later became my dissertation chair). This seminar course was designed for mostly doctoral students in education, but the professor reserved several seats for Harvard Law and Kennedy School students each term due to the popularity of the course. The professor was known to use the Socratic Method, and enjoyed discussion and debate, occasionally "cold-calling" on students to provide their perspective on complex policy matters in education. The final assignment involved a political analysis of an education issue of our choice. I chose to take a historical look at the Chicano Walkouts/Blowouts of 1968 throughout the Southwestern United States. Using original data sources from the Harvard library system (one of the many benefits of attending Harvard was the expansive resources available to students, and the library's ability to acquire materials from other institutions), I used a concentrated-distributed, cost-benefit, political analysis of the Walkouts/Blowouts, and examined the effectiveness of the walkouts from the perspectives of various stakeholders—elected officials, educators, youth, and community members. I was also particularly intrigued by the processes that led to political action by the youth and community members involved in the movement. I realized that the conditions that manifested in my K–12 experiences in the 1980s and 1990s were no different 30 years earlier in the 1960s during the Walkouts/Blowouts in East Los Angeles and across the Southwest. As I began to take a telescopic look back home to the IE from the cold winters of the Northeast while at Harvard, I learned that the statistics were still grim. What was particularly notable was the fact that 50% of the students at my alma mater high school and similar schools in the region, dropped out before graduating. I found a disturbingly low college-going rate, and the percentage of people of color between 24 and 28 years of age with a college degree was among the lowest in the nation. Then I began to ask: If the educational conditions were equally grim during my high school years, why did we not walk out of high school?

Fast forward a few semesters later, and I took a Critical Theory and Pedagogy course with Dr. Eileen de Los Reyes. She encouraged us to conduct an investigation on the origins of a concept of our choice, and I chose "consciousness." For me, I began to wonder how the youth in 1968 walkouts came to build that critical consciousness that led them to organize and actually walk out. Upon reflection, I realized that consciousness was the missing element in my own experiences in high school. I realized that because of my domesticated experiences in school, my ability to develop a critical consciousness was impossible to formulate in school. While there were many moments of resistance in school throughout my K–12 experiences, they were too disconnected and sporadic to form a critical consciousness (that would later manifest itself in college). In fact, my consciousness was probably more critically shaped by my experiences in my neighborhood. That is, being socialized as a male in the 1980s, hanging out with my friends, and the daily struggle to get to and from school by dodging gangs, drugs, and the everyday risks of urban boyhood significantly shaped my consciousness, particularly in middle and high school.

Nonetheless, I delved deeply into the concept of consciousness, and at the same time found myself immersed in my dissertation. I began to grow a cultural connection with the Dominican, Puerto Rican, and Black communities in the Northeast, as the parallels between our experiences were incredibly similar. I saw youth of color constantly struggle to forge their own identity and have to negotiate and sometimes compromise or substitute their street identity with their school identity. When youth were unable to negotiate this ongoing battle for identity, they likely resisted the school environment, and were quickly (or slowly) "exported," as Michelle Fine would say, from school.

I also observed that many youth went to school looking for something. They sought meaning, purpose, and sometimes a chance to start over again, particularly in the alternative and/or continuation school context. For the youth across Boston, particularly those in middle and high schools, they were looking for some kind of recognition. They sought acknowledgment in various ways—some needed basic, relational recognition. But for others, the recognition was far deeper and required more attention. Some wanted recognition in the curriculum and learning experience. Others needed to be recognized through the historical, social, psychological, economic, and political realities of the community. And for others, recognition was exercised by an acknowledgment that education and attending school actually played a vital role in their lives. For many of the students who grew up in this complex social, political, and economic environment, education was, and continues to be, that gateway to opportunity, and in some cases, a life-or-death situation.

What I came to realize is that recognition is the gateway to developing that critical consciousness that manifested itself during the 1968 student walkouts. Students were able to see their own lives, because the people that surrounded them legitimized their very existence. That is, community members who shared their strife affirmed students' complaints about discrimination or corporal punishment in school, mostly because they had similar experiences in school. The curriculum, pedagogical processes, policies, and educational landscape in general were fraught with contradictions (Anyon, 1980). The contradictions were evident through their daily experiences, but also by the larger, national narrative about the availability of opportunity and access through acquiring an education. But the students eventually came to see and experience the cracks in the system that eventually contributed to an awakening of their consciousness and inspiration for their action to improve the system.

These analyses, reflections, and insights led to a series of connections that prompted the question: In what ways are students recognized in their schools? At first, this question revolved around the complex nature of the student-teacher dynamic. In fact, my dissertation largely revolved around the nuances of student-teacher relationships in school, and the subtleties brought about by race, history, class, community, and power in the presence or absence of those relationships. The extent to which students had meaningful and authentic (Valenzuela, 1999) relationships and connections was a major part of their experience. But I later discovered the intersections between recognition and relationships with curriculum, pedagogy, context, and the purpose of education. These observations led to the Praxis of Recognition framework (Rodriguez, 2012).

This framework began to inform my future research agenda by explicitly engaging schools and communities in ways that deliberately facilitated recognition in our school system. Because school dropout is a process-driven, sociological, and political phenomenon, practicing or not practicing recognition is not only an endeavor that can be studied and evaluated, but is a process that is laden with individual agency, opportunity, and power. In other words, recognition is a struggle, and in some cases, it is a battle. It is a struggle between those who understand this dynamic and those who do not. It is a struggle between those who practice recognition and those who do not. It is an ongoing struggle, because most of our schools are not set up in a way that encourages, understands, rewards, or learns from recognition. The culture of our institutions fails miserably in this area, even in the face of decades of empirical research that shows that recognition matters deeply for all students, particularly for low-income students of color.

This book is specifically for educators, advocates, policy makers, and researchers who are particularly concerned with and/or serve low-income communities of color. These communities face particular challenges that require particular responses and solutions. While we know that student-teacher relationships matter, they are hardly a priority in our struggling institutions. While we know that student voice matters and can serve as a strategy to hook students back into school, our institutions dodge this by ignoring it, punishing it, lacking the skill to do something with it, or simply not knowing where to start. We know that learning from role models matters tremendously for youth, particularly those who lack the critical social and cultural capital that is valued by our educational institutions, yet schools largely miss the mark in cultivating these skills. And, we also know that our students bring powerful forms of capital through cultural wealth that largely goes unrecognized (Yosso, 2005). All together, elements such as relationships, voice, and listening to the silent canary is what this book is about; these are some of the elements of institutional culture that play a vital role in perpetuating or resisting dropout.

Thus, this book draws upon lessons learned over the past 10 years of work, particularly from a series of Participatory Action Research (PAR) initiatives that aimed to engage in the struggle for recognition with youth, schools, and communities. Chapter 1 provides context for the dropout crisis, and some perspective as to why we keep missing the mark as stakeholders in the field in education. Chapter 2 proposes the PUEDES approach based on years of research that aims to transform how we understand and respond to the dropout crisis on research, policy, and practical levels. Chapter 2 also applies the PUEDES framework to the experiences of one student—Ramon. Ramon was a student in one of my projects who represents thousands of youth across the country. Chapter 3 describes several projects that triggered the lessons learned, particularly the PROS project in Boston, the POWER project in Miami, and The PRAXIS Project in Southern California. All of these initiatives contributed to vital insights about school culture—largely from the voices and experiences of Black and Latina/o students—and how it contributes to school dropout and/or promotes student engagement. Chapter

4 addresses each of these elements through a nationwide "10-Point Plan to Respond to the Dropout Crisis" that can inform research, practice, and policy at the local level. The book culminates with Chapter 5, which proposes a Theory of Action and a series of reflections and recommendations for action to curb the dropout rate, promote student engagement and success, and ensure more equitable and socially just outcomes, particularly for historically marginalized communities in the United States.

Acknowledgments

This book project has been a labor of love for many years. First and foremost, I want to thank the young people who have allowed me into their lives over the last decade. These include young people from Boston, Miami, and most recently, The Inland Empire or "IE." Your stories, voices, and humanity have taught me "it is never too late." Too many educators, policymakers, and others who claim to be committed to serving our children believe that if we do not catch them by kindergarten, we are too late. I do not buy that. I resist this mainstream belief because I have witnessed struggle, resistance, and victory when the individual agency of young people is met with support, mentorship, and consistency. I have learned that no child ever succeeds or fails in isolation. With every victory, there is usually a group of people who helped make it possible—parents, teachers, coaches, counselors, school leaders, community nonprofits, and other stakeholders.

I also want to thank the many intellectual sources of support that have influenced my thinking over the last decade. Specifically, I would like to thank Pedro Noguera, Gilberto Conchas, Diego Vigil, Eileen de los Reyes, Lisa Delpit, Bob Moses, Joanne Wynne, Danny Solorzano, Richard Elmore, Gary Orfield, Eleanor Drago-Severson, Angela Valenzuela, Mark Warren, Tara Brown, Frank Tuitt, Antonio Cediel, Eduardo Mosqueda, Pedro Nava, Dorinda Carter, Hal Smith, Ambrizeth Lima, Lionel Howard, David Chavez, and Mary Texeira. I would also like to thank two people from my community-college years who had a tremendous impact on my life. The first is Mrs. Calderon who taught History 101. I never had a chance to develop a one-on-one relationship with her, but her enthusiasm for teaching and commitment to student voice in the classroom was very influential to my development as an education researcher and scholar. I would also like to acknowledge Laura Gomez, a counselor and selfless mentor to thousands of young Chicanos/Latinos at San Bernardino Valley College. I am sure that Laura is personally responsible for the success of thousands of us who emerge from the community, and who are committed to serve.

I would also like to thank members of my research team over the years, especially those from the Harvard Graduate School of Education, Martin Wasserberg, from Florida International University, and all of the student-researchers and support team from California State University, San Bernardino, especially Felix Zuniga, Martha Diaz-Zuniga, Karina Aguirre, Mike Arteaga, Priscilla Gutierrez, Lydia Delgado, Stephan Silveira, and Olivia Guerrero. I would also like to thank the leadership at "Martinez High School" for their support, and for the numerous Martinez alumni and community stakeholders who simply care about the current and future condition of our students and community. Their commitment to the community ensures a future of equity and opportunity for generations to come.

Finally, I would like to thank my family. My parents, Louis and Elba, have been a foundation of support for my education ever since I started to dream big as a little Chicano from Colton/San Bernardino. I love you and thank you. I also want to thank my brothers Eddie and Eric for their support and patience as I continue to commit myself to the communities that need the most support—where we are from. I also want to thank my extended family especially my aunts and uncles and cousins who have been there whenever I needed inspiration, support, or some music to keep me focused and motivated. Last but not least, I want to thank Lilly for your unwavering support and belief that I can get this done. Your ability to manage your career, support our family, and inspire my career has been incredible. You are my biggest cheerleader, and you provide me with the best critique when I need it. I love you and thank you for the incredible woman you are and partner in life. I also want to acknowledge my own children. They currently attend the very schools that I am writing about. The struggle and hope I research is also the struggle and hope that I live through my children's experiences in school everyday. This is for them, and for the thousands of children and families we will meet along the way who hope to be inspired in school and catapulted onto a pathway to academic achievement, college success, and a life of opportunity, purpose, and dignity.

Louie F. Rodríguez
San Bernardino, CA
February 13, 2013

The author is grateful for the permission to use the following previously published material:

Rodriguez, L. F. (2013). The PUEDES Approach: Understanding and Responding to the Latina/o Dropout Crisis in the U.S. Special thanks to the *Journal of Critical Thought and Praxis*.

CHAPTER ONE

Unveiling the Hostility and Getting Situated in the Dropout Problem

It was the Spring quarter of 2010 and The PRAXIS project just spent the previous six months in the classroom at Martinez High School. The student-researchers we engaged were excited and ready to present their research findings and solutions to confront the 50% dropout rate at Martinez. The entire school staff including teachers, administrators, janitors, counselors, coaches, and classroom aides filled the audience, and we attended at the invitation of the school principal who opened the doors to The PRAXIS Project. As an alumnus of Martinez about 20 years pri or and from my own observations over the previous six months, I noticed some disturbingly familiar realities. Not only did these observations mirror what I experienced as a former student at Martinez two decades prior, but also reflected what I had seen as a researcher in Boston and Miami. Students reported a rift between them and teachers, students did not feel as though adults listened to them, and many students felt that much of their time in class was spent on meaningless or altogether absent instruction. The students who did identify rich experiences were certainly in the minority; and the strong, committed, and effective teachers flew under, around, or completely off the radar. The experience and result of the presentation was like nothing I had ever witnessed before, particularly toward youth.

Four student-research groups were scheduled to present on dropouts, teaching quality, teacher pedagogy, and the impact of the budget cuts on student engagement. The first group addressed teacher quality and the role of teachers in the lives of students. After administering 120 surveys to 9th and 12th graders, not one student attributed their own motivation in school to their teachers. After hearing this finding, the crowd of mostly teachers reacted with hostility. Many of the audience members responded with side chatter, laughter, and some expletive comments, such as, "This is bullshit" and "I don't have to hear this shit." The PRAXIS team sat shocked. The student-researchers who were still in front of the room and trying to complete their presentation looked at me and said, "What should we do?" Not expecting this response, we began to shush the crowd. I said, "Keep going, you are doing great." Many members of the PRAXIS team became upset.

The student-researchers continued with their presentation, and the principal proceeded to make an announcement after the third student presentation. Because the contract day ended at 3:30 p.m. and there is no obligation for teachers to stay after that time, a significant percentage of teachers left, even when the principal urged teachers to stay and hear the last presentation. Ironically, the presentation focused on stellar teachers and excellence in teaching. While we understood that many teachers have family obligations and maybe previous commitments, many of the students were upset that many teachers left. Obviously aware of the mass exodus from the room, one student-researcher from the last group said, "I appreciate those of you that stayed to hear our presentation. I'm offended that many teachers left and that kind of disrespect is unacceptable." He continued, "Teachers are supposed to be setting an example for us. All those little comments and snickering they made is not a very good example. It's actually pretty shocking."

We later learned that the teachers who actually stayed for the duration were the teachers who were already known by students and administrators to be supportive. This is not to suggest that the teachers who left are unsupportive, but the impression left an imprint on many of the students that day.

Shortly after the presentation, the principal, partner teacher, school board, and superintendent received a slew of e-mails from teachers complaining about the findings and methodologies used in the project. A brief time later, I was contacted by the superintendent and school-board president, who remained steadfastly supportive. They urged The PRAXIS Project to continue. A few days later, letters of support and encouragement were sent by many supportive teachers. Some teachers who initially responded negatively had a "change of heart." They admitted that they initially responded through emotion, rather than recognizing the amazing research and intellectual work the student-researchers presented. Some noted,

> rather than being defensive, we [the school] should celebrate the high level work the students presented and use this as an opportunity to listen to the voices and perspectives of the students. There is no other opportunity [for us] to hear the students.

In addition to teachers, some parents of the students who presented heard about the presentation. I was contacted and given full support by parents who were proud of their sons' and daughters' participation, and firmly believed that students should be given the opportunity to share their perspectives and experiences in school. Two parents began to attend research-team meetings and our public presentations across the community as a gesture of support.

As someone who had led two previous projects in different parts of the country, I had never encountered such a response. This was troubling given the challenges facing the school. We were there to confront the 50% dropout rate facing this school. I was also keenly aware that the ways in which institutions function directly contribute to this ongoing problem, and that they have the responsibility to respond to this problem. I reflected on this experience in many ways, but one was apparent. The way the students were received that day was a direct reflection of the school culture. It is also critical to note that many supportive teachers seemed fearful of expressing their support for our efforts in a public setting. As researchers of school culture, we understand that there are strong, internal school dynamics that create conditions that prevent certain perspectives from being heard.

While our intent was and continues to be constructive in our engagement with schools and communities, this experience helped us understand that the voices, experiences, and ideas generated by students will not always be welcomed. Some educators are simply not ready to listen and learn; others find students' voices and insights refreshing, and a much needed opportunity to listen to the people they serve. Upon reflection and further engagement with the school, we made every next step deliberately and strategically so this gesture of hostility would not happen again. The next public presentation was drastically different.

A Community's Love

After the 2010–2011 school year (year 2), we decided to present our findings to a more inclusive group of people, specifically, the school and the larger community. With the support of the Martinez principal and district superintendent, we invited everyone including Martinez faculty and staff, students, parents, grandparents, Martinez alumni, elected officials, city officials, professional educators, school board members from Martinez and beyond, nonprofit leaders, and business leaders.

The goals of the community event were multifold:

(1) To have students engage the community in a dialogue about their research findings;
(2) To have students present three awards to exemplary Martinez teachers;
(3) To engage the community and alumni in possibilities of interacting with and supporting Martinez;
(4) To create networking opportunities among Martinez students, faculty, staff, administrators, and various community stakeholders, and;
(5) To provide a space for community members to share testimonies about ways to improve Martinez.

The reception at this event was starkly different from our presentation a year earlier. Parents, grandparents, siblings, alumni, and other community stakeholders were explicitly supportive of this work. After the students presented their research on teacher quality, dropouts, and school policy, students were praised and the audience was eager to ask questions. Students felt affirmed, recognized, and respected. Parents were in tears, and two different families approached members of the research team in utter disbelief, astounded by their son's or daughter's engagement, interest, and leadership within the project. One parent stated, "I've never seen my son so excited about something in school. This is really great. Thank you." Another parent said, "I didn't know my son was capable of speaking in public. I'm very proud of him." Students gave testimonies about their experiences with the project, parents in tears shared how proud they were of their children, and community members affirmed the work as critical to the advancement of the community.

Students in The PRAXIS Project also generated three awards as a gesture to recognize exemplary teachers at Martinez. The awards included The Most Caring Teacher, The Most Committed Teacher, and The Most Creative Teacher. During the presentation, some of the recipients showed tears of appreciation and joy. We later learned that the school, much like most schools, does not institute any formal recognition of teachers. For one of the teachers, this was the first formal recognition she had been given by students in her 10-plus years as a teacher.

Finally, we provided an opportunity for community members to dialogue. We learned that Martinez alumni were represented in the audience from every decade going back to the 1940s. Everyone in attendance was in awe and inspired by the community's continued willingness to serve and support The PRAXIS Project and Martinez High. Community leaders, including a dean of students at a local university, a retired dentist, and a champion of educational opportunity throughout the K–20 pipeline, who all happened to be Martinez alumni, praised the students and the research efforts, and encouraged continuous community-school collaboration. The hostile reception a year earlier was transformed into an embracement from the community, filled with love, recognition, and hope.

These two distinct experiences present a power struggle between institutional culture and community engagement, and its impact on student engagement and disengagement, especially in the context of the dropout crisis. One does not operate without the other, but a veil of deceit that detaches the two will emerge if we allow it. We realized that schools are sitting on a wealth of untapped community resources and history. We also realized that the research and insights shared by the students were confirmed by the behavior of the adults during the presentation. When students fail to see motivation through their teachers, it is apparent why. When the students feel as though the teachers will not listen, it is apparent why. When the students say that their teachers do not motivate them, it is apparent why. Yet, while these realities do not and should not be used to paint Martinez High with such a broad stroke, these experiences largely encompass the student-experience narrative, and help explain why the perspectives from the teachers who dissent from this counterproductive view go unregistered, at least in public. We learned that a significant number of teachers do recognize, do engage, and do work for equity and social justice every day in the classroom. It was critically important to realize that these voices either continue to fall on deaf ears, or are silenced by the culture of schools.

This experience was also an indication of the lack of attention given to the dropout crisis facing Martinez. Any review of the numbers shows that approximately 1,200 freshmen enter each year, but the numbers of students who walk across the graduation stage four years later hovers around 500. If the adults within the school rejected students' attributions associated with their own motivation, why would they confront such a troubling fact facing the school?

But Martinez is not alone. In the region, state, and the country, schools like Martinez are present and open for business every day. Schools like Martinez fit a particular profile. They are predominantly attended by low-income Black and Latina/o students; they have a sizeable English Learner population; they are underresourced; there is a significant underrepresentation of teachers of color; there are problems with suspensions and expulsions, particularly among males of color; and the culture of the schools rejects and avoids critical conversations on topics that are typically relevant to address or respond to the various challenges. Rather than talking about equity, relevance, and excellence, they talk about what they continue to lack, the next round of assessments, and the pervasive dominance of policy and rules that typically dictate how they act.

Our schools, the systems that are meant to support them, and the larger institutions that prepare teachers, leaders, counselors, other practitioners, and policy makers, have failed to comprehensively understand and respond to the dropout crisis. We spend too much time, energy, and resources on systems, and too little time on what happens within those institutions. We spend an exorbitant amount of time, energy, and resources on testing, rather than investing in what it takes to achieve and excel in our institutions. And we spend such an incredible amount of time demonizing teachers, sidestepping

the social and cultural realities of communities, and ignoring inequities that
are perpetuated by and through the system that we have failed to respond deliberately to this national crisis. The fate of our economy and political stability as a nation is dependent on an educated polity with the most simple and
fundamental credential. We know it as the high school diploma. However,
the diploma alone will not cure all of the social ills that contribute to the
dropout crisis. Yet responding to the education crisis facing mostly children
and communities of color through the dropout crisis will point us toward
some of the most pressing and critical inroads that can push our schools,
communities, and country into the 21st century with equity, dignity, and
hope.

A Snapshot of the Dropout Crisis

The statistics reflecting the dropout and/or pushout crisis are sobering (U.S.
Department of Education, 2011). Whereas 70% of all U.S. students who enter high school will graduate four years later, only about half of all low-
income students of color will graduate (Balfanz & Legters, 2004; Graduate
Summit Report, 2012). For the latter, for every 100 entering Black and
Latina/o high school freshmen, roughly 50 will actually graduate four years
later. Research continues to show that the dropout crisis is concentrated in
residentially and educationally segregated communities that tend to be primarily poor, Black and Latina/o, and are typically characterized by high rates
of English Learners and immigrant students (Orfield, Losen, & Wald, 2004).
This form of concentrated inequality is particularly concerning when Lati-
nas/os, in particular, are the youngest and fastest-growing racial-minority
group in the country (Rodriguez, 2008; U.S. Census Bureau, 2003). The results of a recent report also showed that in districts with a disproportionate
number of Latina/o and/or African American students, $1,000 less is spent
per student on their public education (Spatig-Amerikaner, 2012). Thus, the
issue of school completion and its relationship with pervasive and concentrated inequities remain major civil rights issues in the United States, particularly as the K through 12 population becomes more diverse in the 21st
century (Fry & Lopez, 2012).

    To grasp the enormity of the Latina/o student presence in U.S. public
schools specifically, three million Latinos are born each year, and 20,000 Latinos turn 18 each month. It is also known that one in four babies born in the
United States is Latina/o, and over 90% of all Latina/o kindergartners are
U.S. born. In California, for example, half of all children in the public
schools are Latina/o, and in some districts and schools, 99% of the student
population is Latina/o. Furthermore, demographic change is occurring in ar-

eas across the United States that is not consistent with historical trends. For instance, two of the fastest-growing regions of Latino population and English Learner growth are Tennessee and Utah (Gandara & Contreras, 2009). These demographic trends only amplify the work by economists, sociologists, and policy analysts who continue to find that dropouts not only have a major impact on the social, political, and economic well-being of society, but also on the quality of life and vitality for communities that have faced this reality for decades.

Despite the presence of the so-called dropout "crisis," neither public policy nor educational practice has responded with great fervor. With the exception of President Obama's State of the Union address in January 2012, where he called for raising the age to leave school from 16 to 18 years, and a sprinkling of conferences addressing the issue, the education discourse in the United States continues to be dominated by the impact of budget cuts on local schools, merit pay for teachers based on test scores, and the implementation of the Common Core standards. There remains a lingering incongruence between the real challenges facing particularly low-income, urban schools and communities and the ways in which we have responded as a society, particularly around the dropout and/or pushout crisis.

Yet, there is a preponderance of empirical research over the last 20 years that helps explain why the dropout rate is so high (Rumberger & Rodriguez, 2011). Research has shown that individual risk factors, poverty, institutional factors, and student-teacher relationships are vital to understanding why students drop out or stay in school (Rumberger, 2012; Valenzuela, 1999). This framework will be addressed and built upon in Chapter 2. Research also shows that fourth-grade reading and math scores and student attendance and behavior in the sixth grade are strong predictors of school failure (or success) and dropout by the end of high school (Balfanz, Herzog, & Mac Iver, 2007). Research also shows that teachers have a tremendous impact on student development and success in and beyond the classroom (Ferguson, 2003). Research also suggests that the implementation of high-stakes, standardized testing has contributed to an increase in dropout rates, even shortly after NCLB (No Child Left Behind) was implemented (Meier & Wood, 2004). In fact, punitive policies and practices such as testing and disciplinary approaches have proven to be counterproductive, particularly for low-income students of color in high-poverty schools and communities, and this has also contributed to the looming dropout crisis in the United States (Yang, 2009). Such policies and practices result in a school-to-prison pipeline, rather than a school-to-college and/or career pipeline.

Despite the research, educational policy and practice have fallen short in responding to the crisis, particularly in schools such as Martinez High School in urban southern California, mentioned in the introduction to this chapter. At Martinez, like many middle and high schools in its region, over 90% of the 3,400 students are students of color, and just over 80% of the students are Latina/o students, including a 30% English Learner population. Once labeled a "California Distinguished School" in the late 1980s, Martinez High has faced waves of school violence, frequent changes in school leadership, and a 50% dropout rate for years. Upon a review of the entering freshman enrollment rates in comparison to graduating seniors four years later, 530 students out of 1100 actually graduated on time in 2009, which was the spring before I began The PRAXIS Project at Martinez. While this suggests a 50%-plus dropout rate, the district reported a less than 10% dropout rate. When officials were asked about this reality, the whereabouts for most of the missing students were simply "unknown." Further, while there are promising programs scattered across the United States that are meant to respond to schools such as Martinez High, we have yet to see large-scale policy initiatives aimed at this national and localized crisis.

Some Reasons Why School Culture and Dropout Have Not Been Introduced to One Another

The reasons why the dropout crisis looms and goes unaddressed in any significant way are complex and multifaceted. There are at least five key reasons that keep practitioners, researchers, policy makers, and communities away from getting at the core of understanding and action around the dropout crisis, particularly in low-income Black and Latina/o communities. They are:

(1) Methodology used to examine dropout;
(2) Epistemology or knowledge orientation used to understand the dropout problem;
(3) A reform perspective that overemphasizes structures and systems rather than the culture of those institutions;
(4) An overwhelming fear of implicating the role that schools do play in perpetuating or resisting the crisis, and;
(5) Overwhelming emphasis on a deficit orientation toward youth, schools, and communities that steers us away from examining what actually works in schools.

The Problem With Research Methodology

Researchers and dropout research have failed to provide more thorough models for understanding and analyzing the dropout crisis. Dropping out of school is a complex process, rather than a one time decision or occurrence. However, studies on dropout have implicated important school processes such as relationships, engagement, and the role of connectedness in keeping students in school (Nieto, 1999), yet, consequential studies and policy seem to lack such elements. Part of the problem is that the conceptual frames evolving out of the mostly quantitative studies on dropout make it analytically challenging to use a frame of "relationships," for instance, to analyze what is going on in schools. This is due largely to the sole use of survey data, which has not yielded complex frameworks that help researchers study and understand how and why school processes, specifically, contribute to student engagement and disengagement in school. Conversely, while a notable few have provided powerful frames for studying dropout—such as Fine's use of "exporting dissent" and Valenzuela's authentic and aesthetic notions of caring—more work is needed to both theorize and provide process-oriented explanations as to why and how students drop out of school. Also lacking is a grounded, empirically driven, and relevant model that guides research and analysis directly into the role that schools play, particularly in schools serving low-income Black and Latina/o students where the problem is most pervasive. While heavily quantitative studies have gleaned important insights into the various individual and systemic factors that do correlate with dropout (Rumberger, 2004), only qualitative studies rooted in complex, conceptual frameworks will help push the methodological and process-driven understanding of the dropout crisis. Through grounded, context-specific, and critical frameworks that privilege the experiences, voices, and perspectives of the individuals and communities affected, researchers and research will be able to understand and uncover the nuances associated with school culture, such as student-teacher relationships, student voice, and the complex nature of excellence. PUEDES, discussed in Chapter 2, aims to address this absence in the dropout literature.

The Narrow Nature of Epistemology in the Dropout Discourse

Another dimension to methodology is epistemology. Elsewhere, I have argued that framing and understanding the dropout crisis from a school culture perspective is partially a function of the fundamental knowledge orientation of the researcher examining the phenomenon (Brown & Rodriguez, 2009). That is, as the number of critical scholars and perspectives emerging in the academy increases, the frameworks and methodological orientations begin to become more complex and insightful, especially as these scholars are able to compliment their research eye with personal, political, and intellectual lenses that provide deeper insight into the phenomenon under study (Foley & Valenzuela, 2005). In other words, like all research, the researcher matters. Just in the last few years, a series of more relevant frameworks have emerged that include Critical Race and Chicana feminist perspectives, which help explore and explain critical social and cultural processes in schools (Huber Perez, 2009; Rodriguez & Brown, 2009; Yosso, 2005). These frameworks are able to draw out different types of knowledge and understanding that, in part, privilege the voices, experiences, and perspectives that are typically overlooked in education research. This is in direct contradistinction to previous studies on dropout that tend to focus on traditional explanations such as curriculum, policy, and individual effort (Ladson-Billings, 2000; Huber Perez, 2009). The PUEDES framework aims to expand upon these critical frameworks by focusing on those elements that happen in and around schools that resist or perpetuate dropout in schools, particularly in low-income Black and Latina/o communities.

More Culture, Not Structure

Another reason why school culture is overlooked in the study of dropout is because the dominant direction in education reform continues to focus on structures and systems, not the culture of schools (Elmore, 1995). Most simply, structural reform is a dimension to change that focuses solely on the policies or systems (i.e., testing, standards, or the size of a classroom) affecting education, even though education is largely a process-driven endeavor. Some have characterized this type of reform as rearranging the furniture (Elmore, 1995). If the end goal is to have people interact and converse in a living-room setting, for example, rearranging the furniture alone does not guarantee meaningful conversation, interactions, or relationship building. Much more needs to happen, namely a cultural shift for people to actually engage with one another.

In a widely revered analysis of school reform, Elmore (1995) posited three reasons why structural reform persists and continues to fail. The first is the symbolic nature of reform. If education advocates, policy makers, and educators themselves frame the problem on a superficial level, such as class size, then fixing the problem associated with class size will be the end goal. By reducing class size, the decision makers will leave the impression to the outside world that efforts are being made to change or improve the situation, when in reality, only a symbolic action occurred—changing the number of students in each class. The second reason structural reform is so rampant is its relative ease in implementation (Elmore, 1995). It is quite easy to rearrange the furniture in one's living room, but trying to get people to meaningfully engage with one another is a much more complex undertaking. In other words, reducing class size is relatively easy, compared to fundamentally transforming the culture of the classroom. Thirdly, Elmore (1995) argued that stakeholders hold high value over the role that structures (i.e., class size) play in their everyday work. For instance, if a teacher is unable to develop a meaningful relationship with all students, then class size becomes the culprit. Or, if the school is facing a 50% dropout rate, the rationale that is used revolves around how the school's size disables its ability to effectively serve all students, thus falsely blaming the dropout problem on the enrollment level of the school.

The narrow focus on structure and systems is problematic for two reasons. Of course policies, resources, laws, and specifically, school size, curriculum, and local educational policymaking matter tremendously. But they are not the only things that matter. The narrow focus on structure hampers our ability to meaningfully understand the complex nature of the dropout problem. As mentioned, previous research has outlined correlative effects between a student's individual characteristics (race) and structure (living in poverty), and dropping out of school. However, the problem is much more complex than that. Some seasoned or lay analysts often argue that poverty alone is the problem. Others point to social policy alone. The deficit-oriented perspective alone would have us believe that students do not care about or value school, nor do their families or communities. This could not be more wrong. So, an overemphasis on structure alone can easily lead us into a series of misinformed and often racist, classist, or sexist assumptions about particular communities, especially Black and Latina/o communities. An inclusion and an analysis of institutional culture encourages a much more complex understanding of the problem, such as understanding how schools respond to or treat poor Black and Latina/o youth. This is an entirely different way of understanding the dropout crisis, and can lead stakeholders toward a series of implications that are more useful and potentially just. The PUEDES framework outlined in the next chapter helps guide these efforts.

Avoiding Fear and Blame in the Dropout Context

The final reason why school culture has been overlooked or ignored in the dropout research is a culture in the academic and scholarly domain that fears the implication that schools actually do play a role in producing or perpetuating school dropout. As a former middle-school counselor and high-school math teacher during the high-stakes, fear-prone, threat-driven policy climate of the No Child Left Behind era, I am aware that pressure to raise test scores was and continues to be placed on the schools and the teachers serving them, even when the support and resources were promised but were nowhere in sight. And while high-stakes, standardized testing is a purely structural approach to education reform and shown to fail (Meier & Wood, 2004), there is research suggesting that high-performing, high-poverty schools actually do focus on the factors and processes within schools that are central to their high performance (Center for Public Education, 2005; Wehlage & Rutter, 1986). Despite this research, there seems to be a fear or concern that implicating the school ignores and decontextualizes the school from the effects of poverty, or such an analysis is misinterpreted as teacher-bashing. Yet, years of research, such as Ron Edmonds's work on the Effective Schools Movement (Edmonds, 1979a, 1979b; Edmonds & Frederiksen, 1974), suggest that schools matter and are more effective, particularly when characterized by high expectations, a safe and disciplined school environment, and the presence of competent and committed teachers (Pianta, Stuhlman, & Hamre, 2002). Yet, the fear of implicating schools is one that must be met with the use of relevant research and fair critique. After all, educators, policy makers, and the media are quick to blame youth of color, family values, and communities for education failure. Why do we skirt around school culture by focusing on poverty or a student's lack of motivation or focus? In my assessment, it comes down to power. Many stakeholders use deficit-oriented perspectives to justify their inability to adequately serve low-income Black and Latina/o students. Some argue that these youth are incapable of rigorous work, are behavior problems, or do not value education. Education scholars have repeatedly refuted such perspectives for decades (Valencia & Solorzano, 1997; Yosso, 2005). Recognizing the role of schools in resisting or perpetuating school dropout needs to be added to the conceptual explanation addressing the dropout crisis so that the responses and solutions are relevant, rigorous, and complex. The PUEDES framework provides a vehicle for engaging in that type of analysis and understanding in order to curb dropout and design equitable responses.

The pervasive struggle to curb the dropout rate, especially in those schools serving low-income and historically marginalized communities, such as Latinas/os and African Americans, is due in part to the methodological and epistemological nature of research, and the misguided nature of structurally driven school reform efforts. Sometimes well-intentioned efforts are focused too much on programming and not on what happens in those programs. At other times there is too much emphasis on raising standards or the achievement targets, and not enough emphasis on the processes involved in helping students and teachers meet those targets. Attention to structural changes alone, or blam-

ing the most vulnerable youth or communities for their own demise, only per-
petuates mechanistic and technical reform efforts, rather than meaningful ges-
tures toward real, positive change (Bartolome, 1994, 2002; Trueba, 1999). To
address these questions, an approach to reform that focuses on the culture of
the institution, or school culture, must be centralized.

The Significance of School Culture

For at least 40 years, there has been a shadowed narrative in the field of education about the role of school culture in shaping meaningful change (Payne,
2008; Sarason, 1972). However, this narrative has been far less recognized
than perhaps the structurally driven education research, probably for the reasons noted by Elmore's (1995) analysis mentioned earlier in this chapter.
When it comes to the dropout research specifically, school culture has been
largely overlooked due to methodological and epistemological reasons
(Brown & Rodriguez, 2009). That is, a true commitment to stopping and re-
versing the dropout crisis facing the United States will require a series of
recommendations that are research-based and centered directly on the practices, processes, and policies that shape and are shaped by school culture. In
fact, these elements of school culture are largely responsible for facilitating
student engagement and disengagement in school; however, they are the
most ignored and least recognized and addressed.

School culture refers to the values, beliefs, and processes that characterize institutional life. School culture within high schools, for instance, is defined by the social climate within the school (i.e., who does and does not get
along with whom), the normative beliefs and practices (i.e., whether students' voices are heard and considered in decision-making), and the modes
of communication and interactions among the various people within a school
(i.e., the nature of student-teacher relationships). Elsewhere, I have defined
school culture as the place where identities are forged, where meaning is negotiated, and most simply, "how things get done" (Rodriguez, 2008).

In addition to including school culture into a framework to arrive at a
more complex understanding of the dropout crisis, it is equally important to
understand the roles that race, class, gender, power and knowledge, language, and the purpose of schooling play as well (Oakes & Rogers, 2006;
Rodriguez, 2011; Solorzano & Yosso, 2001). When considering the dropout
crisis and Latina/o and Black students specifically, frameworks informed by
Critical Race Theory and LatCrit are especially relevant, as they provide a
framework for understanding how race, racism, language, immigration
status, and identity inform the process of dropping out of school. In addition,
critical research perspectives from Critical Theory and Critical Pedagogy are

also informative, as they deepen an understanding of school dropout by providing a language of critique of schools as perpetuating inequality and at the same time instilling hope, particularly in the most marginalized communities in the United States (Cassidy & Bates, 2005; de los Reyes & Gozemba, 2001; Lauria & Mirón, 2005).

It is vital to situate these critical frameworks within the context of education reform and school culture specifically because of the sanitized discourse that dominates the field. For instance, topics of curriculum, assessment, and other structural elements such as policy are often discussed in a decontextualized manner that ignores the social, political, economic, cultural, and historical realities of the students, communities, and the system. This discourse is also accompanied by a "good will" assumption that these "change" efforts are good for the youth and their communities. There is little critical analysis about the inherent racist, classist, sexist, or let-us-help-these-poor-kids mentality that often informs these efforts. When the discussion is kept at the "we-are-going-to-help-these-kids-because-we-know-what-is-right-for-them" level, there is hardly any discussion about the intentions behind these efforts or their viability in a culturally, linguistically, and economically diverse community; and there is hardly any discussion about the social and cultural dimensions to schooling that are vital to the development of student engagement or disengagement, such as student-teacher relationships, learning from the experiences of marginalized students, or engaging in a Praxis of Recognition (Rodriguez, 2012). These will be addressed in Chapter 4 and Chapter 5, as specific elements of school culture that are vital to shaping the engagement and disengagement of students, particularly Black and Latina/o youth.

In order to devise a more rigorous and relevant framework for understanding and responding to the dropout crisis, the PUEDES approach was developed. This approach not only pushes for a better understanding of the conditions that shape dropout in Black and Latina/o communities, but can also be used to guide equitable responses to the dropout crisis. PUEDES builds upon previous education research, and argues that it can also be used to examine other educational phenomena at a complex level of depth and rigor. The power of the PUEDES approach is brought to life through the experiences of Ramon, a case study of a Latina/o high school student who attended a school that struggled to understand him and keep him engaged. PUEDES is used as an analytical framework for understanding Ramon's situation, and also for identifying potential intervention points that were missed or overlooked. Ramon's experiences represent the thousands of students I had the privilege of working with in Boston, Miami, and now Southern California, who struggled to stay in school.

CHAPTER TWO

Prioritizing Institutional Culture: Proposing the PUEDES Approach to Understand and Respond to the Dropout Crisis

Dropping out of school has been historically explained through two primary lenses:

(1) Dropping out as a result of the structural conditions of schools, such as poverty or unsuccessful and/or irrelevant policy, or

(2) Through the (in)actions or characteristics of students themselves (Rumberger, 2012).

This chapter proposes a research-driven and conceptually rigorous framework that centralizes the role that school culture plays in reducing and resisting dropout (Conchas, 2001; Conchas & Rodriguez, 2007; Elmore, 1995). This framework also builds upon the way research, policy, and practice has been used to understand and respond to the dropout crisis (Brown & Rodriguez, 2009; Datnow, Hubbard, & Mehan, 2002; Mehan & Wood, 1975). The interactive nature of PUEDES not only centralizes the role of institutional culture, but also provides a degree of depth and complexity that pushes stakeholders to understand and respond through solutions that are incisive, relevant, and practical (Rodriguez, 2013).

The dearth of equitable responses is partially related to the ways in which researchers, practitioners, and policy makers have examined and understood the dropout and/or pushout issue. In other words, we lack a complex and contextually specific analysis of the dropout and/or pushout crisis. This is partially related to the lack of critical tools or frameworks available to discuss, analyze, and respond to the dropout crisis. Much of the existing work on the crisis continues to focus on statistical associations between particular factors and characteristics and one's likelihood of dropping out of school. And while such work has gleaned critical insight into the challenges facing the crisis, this work leaves much to speculation and much to discover. Interestingly, the processes and practices that one would presume matter, may very likely be among the most useful in helping us understand, explain, and respond to the dropout and/or pushout crisis. In fact, there are likely to be processes and practices that shape the dropout process that may not be measurable by traditional research approaches. This calls for an analytical lens that incorporates these perspectives.

Beyond the research, district policymakers, school leadership, and teachers'-lounge talk often fail to do justice to the complexity associated with the problem. In a worst-case scenario, educators, policymakers, and the general public are more likely to engage in deficit-oriented discussions about the crisis where blame is placed on students, their families, and their communities for not having the right values or priorities. Such perspectives tend to be too oversimplistic, such as "if only they would just care a little more about education." The proposed framework in this chapter aims to assist the research community, policymakers, and practitioners in generating more deliberate responses that are equitable and just, particularly for and with communities disproportionately impacted by the dropout crisis. The proposed framework is not just another analytical tool; rather, it is both concerned with a deeper and more robust analysis of the dropout and/or pushout crisis *so* that we can respond more equitably. Thus, the PUEDES approach is driven by the notion that schools indeed matter, and that dropping out of school is not solely a function of poverty or individual will alone, but likely to be a far more complex process requiring a much more complex and comprehensive response.

In this chapter, an overview of how the dropout problem has been historically understood is discussed, followed by some thoughts about what is missing in the analysis. Then the Paradigm to Understand and Examine Dropout and Engagement in Society (PUEDES) approach is described. PUEDES demonstrates that together, social structures, institutional culture, and individual agency explain how and why school dropout is so prevalent among low-income students of color. PUEDES builds upon the theoretical groundings and findings from a larger qualitative study that examined Latino students' experiences during the dropout process (Rodriguez & Brown, 2009). In this chapter, PUEDES focuses on the operationalization and application of PUEDES by sharing the experiences of a student who I shadowed, interviewed, and learned from over a two-year period. The chapter culminates with a series of implications for stakeholders that uses the PUEDES approach as a tool for devising equitable and relevant responses at the policy and practical levels. While the PUEDES approach does not claim to have discovered the proverbial silver bullet, it does make a bold assertion that PUEDES will push us forward in understanding and in taking action to promote more widespread, equitable access and opportunity, particularly in our nation's most marginalized schools and communities.

Research Context and Conceptual Framework

Before proposing an alternative framework for understanding the dropout crisis in the United States, it is important to recognize the dominant conceptual framework that currently guides how dropout is framed and understood. There are two primary analytical approaches that have been used for understanding school dropout and typically found from research in the quantitative tradition [1]—the *individual perspective* and the *institutional perspective* (Rumberger, 2004). In the first, the problem of school dropout is implicated within students themselves through the so-called "risk factors," such as race, immigration status, language proficiency, poverty level, and (dis)ability, as well as school-related dispositions and behaviors (i.e., whether a student does his homework, skips class, or likes school). The second perspective concerns the problem within institutions (e.g., family, school, or community). Such factors include the composition of the family, a school's size and location, availability of resources, student-body demographics, school-level policies and practices, and a community's poverty level or degree of racial and economic segregation (Fry & Taylor, 2012; Rumberger, 2004).

While the individual-structural frame has helped researchers and other stakeholders understand what factors are associated with a student's likelihood of dropping out, the current framework is incomplete. Russell Rumberger (2004) himself has argued that the individual-structural frame does not allow for an analysis of the role that school processes play in understanding and preventing dropout. Dropout scholars suggest that identifying and disentangling the complex intersection between structural and individual factors is necessary but methodologically challenging (Rodriguez & Brown, 2009; Rumberger, 2004). Research methodology is important to acknowledge because dropout has traditionally been studied using quantitative methods, although there are some notable exceptions (Fine, 1991; Rodriguez & Brown, 2009; Valenzuela, 1999). It is common knowledge that quantitative methodology allows an overview of *what* factors have been significantly associated with dropout; however, *how* and *why* explanations require process-oriented methodologies (Maxwell, 1996; Strauss & Corbin, 1998) that allow researchers to look at the intersections between individual and institutional factors, and allow for an analysis of how school-based processes may or may not contribute to the dropout crisis.

---

1   It is important to acknowledge the methodological approach because it not only impacts the kind of data that is generated, but it also illuminates the epistemological values that guide and inform the results, interpretation, and implications of the study. This topic will resonate well with critical qualitative researchers.

It has been argued that individual and institutional factors are inextricably linked and coconstructed (Brown & Rodriguez, 2009). For example, being poor and Latino (individual risk factors) cannot be isolated from the ways in which schools (structural and cultural factors) respond to poor, Latino students. The institution's response comes in the form of the opportunity landscape across the school (i.e., strong teachers, curriculum options, mentorship, counseling), and the complex ways that students and teachers negotiate that landscape of opportunities (i.e., what people talk about, the quality of relationships, the degree of student voice and leadership opportunities in critical decisions that shape the quality of education they receive). Thus, the fact that majority-Latina/o student high schools fail to offer Latino history courses (structure as curriculum) further exemplifies why so many Latino youth continue to believe that school is boring (individual dispositions), or that they are not learning anything meaningful (Conchas & Rodriguez, 2007). Further, the reasons why a school might be resistant to Latino history courses are fundamentally linked to the cultural fabric of the school and community itself—its values, priorities, norms, and expectations. Additionally, students' dispositions toward school are shaped by their everyday schooling experiences that comprise the structure and culture of the school.

Thus, the idea of "disentangling" the individual and structural factors and processes in schools is a methodological and epistemological problem (Brown & Rodriguez, 2009). The proposed framework in this chapter attempts to address the epistemology of understanding the dropout problem because individual and structural factors and processes are indeed entangled (Brown & Rodriguez, 2009), as described in the example above where policy factors and institutional values influence individual students' dispositions and are also mediated by institutional culture. The methodological challenge lies in the fact that the traditional, quantitative approach disallows an analysis of the school-level processes, such as the role of school culture, community culture, or the culture of society and its role in shaping, facilitating, and understanding dropout. A paradigm that incorporates culture into the traditional individual-structure paradigm and sets the foundation for PUEDES is the structure-culture-agency paradigm.

The Structure-Culture-Agency Paradigm

The structure-culture-agency paradigm (see Mehan & Wood, 1975, for a discussion of the framework's origins) emerged from the notion that social action is a result of the interaction between social structures and human agency, a concept known as structuration by sociologists (Datnow et al., 2002; Giddens, 1984). Most simply, this approach suggests that people act according to the restraints or flexibility of one's environment, either based on the rules and policies (structure) and/or the cultural expectations (culture) that are characteristic of a particular context.

Education scholars applied this perspective to an analysis of school reform and found that culture was a powerful facilitating force in addition to structure and agency (Datnow et al., 2002). In their work, Datnow, Hubbard, and Mehan (2002) found that various dimensions of school culture—teacher ideology and teaching and learning processes—mediated the effectiveness of the reform efforts. They found that deficit-oriented perspectives about students of color and English Learners hindered the implementation of reform efforts because some teachers believed particular students were incapable of meeting the challenges of a newly implemented, rigorous curriculum. The work of these researchers suggests that a teacher's deficit perspectives, for example, may not significantly influence the culture of the school, but a critical mass of deficit perspectives can certainly shape the normative beliefs and practices of a school, thus constructing the school's culture (Ancess, 1998).

Datnow et al. (2002) also found the structure-culture-agency paradigm to be a reflexive and interactional framework where each element influences and is shaped by the other:

> Inasmuch as culture involves power and is the site of social differences and struggles, we believe that culture is of equal importance and profoundly impacts both structure and agency.... Structure and agency work reflexively. So do agency and culture, structure and culture. In the agency of individuals we see structure and culture operating; in culture, we see structure and agency; and in structure, we see agency and culture (Datnow et al., 2002, p. 16).

Therefore, the structure-culture-agency framework not only privileges an interactive analysis of individual with structural factors, as posited by Rumberger (2004), but also encourages an incorporation of culture. The inclusion of culture and the application of the structure-culture-agency framework to education are likely to be the strongest contributions to the PUEDES approach. However, PUEDES differs in that it expands upon the individual concepts of structure, culture, and agency; is applied to rigorously understand the dropout crisis; and demonstrates its analytical strength by also shaping equitable solutions to this pervasive crisis.

The Paradigm to Understand and Examine Dropout
and Engagement in Society (PUEDES) Approach

In an attempt to provide a practical, theoretically grounded, and context-specific framework to better understand the dropout crisis, PUEDES was developed. While PUEDES can directly be applied to understanding dropout, it also can be used as a conceptual framework for understanding various issues in education (i.e., parent engagement, student success, teacher ideology), and as an analytical tool to understand broader social, political, and cultural issues. As stated, PUEDES, like the structure-culture-agency framework, recognizes the significance of structure and agency, but also includes the dimension of culture, particularly in the context of schools or school culture. The PUEDES approach also builds upon the structure-culture-agency framework in many ways, including how:

(1) It expands upon our understanding of the three dimensions (structure, culture, and agency), particularly in the context of dropout,
(2) It acknowledges the inherent, asymmetrical power dynamic of structure, culture, and agency as three practically interrelated but theoretically separate forces,
(3) It provides a far more complex analysis of dropout, particularly in reference to low-income Black and Latina/o students and other students of color who are often blamed for their failure through deficit perspectives, and
(4) It serves as a tool for designing, creating, and envisioning equitable solutions to student disengagement in the context of the dropout crisis.

Understanding the Three Dimensions of the PUEDES Approach

The structure-culture-agency framework outlined by Datnow, McHugh, Stringfield, and Hacker (1998) provided a critical introduction and application of the framework to the field of education. However, there was limited attention placed on the operationalization of structure, culture, and agency. For the purposes of this framework, structure refers to policies, procedures, rules, and resources. Structure also refers to the ways in which people, resources, and space are arranged and distributed in any given environment. Most stakeholders would refer to structure as the "system," and include family as system, school as system, and society as system. Each of these structures has a set of policies, procedures, and rules. In a family, a matriarchal structure may define the family. In school, the formal curriculum and enrollment characteristics help define the school structure, whereas the social structure is comprised of the social policies and poverty concentration in the community or society.

Agency, on the other hand, refers to individual actions, beliefs, and perceptions of one's reality. Agency is probably one of the most implicated reasons why students engage or disengage in school. One's agency is also context-specific, as it may appear different from one context to the next. For instance, a student may exercise his identity at home in one way but in an entirely different way at school. Similarly, one's agency may even change from class to class and teacher to teacher. An active, vocal, and engaged student in history class may appear to be inactive, silent, and disengaged in a math class. The coconstructive nature of the proposed framework below demonstrates that agency is a function of the culture and structure of school (see Figure 2.1).

Figure 2.1. Structure-Agency-Culture

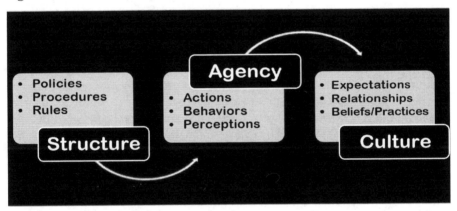

Culture on the other hand, and school culture specifically, refers to the values, beliefs, and processes that characterize institutional life. In schools, school culture is defined by the social climate of the school, the normative beliefs and practices of people within the school, and also is made up of interpersonal and intrapersonal modes of communicating. School culture also

embod[ies] the "boundaries, categories, and rules in which meaning is negotiated" (Lipka, 1998, p. 23) which results in normative, acceptable, and sometimes contentious realities that characterize institutional life—a place where the student finds themselves negotiating their everyday existence...culture is referred to school-level matters associated with expectations, the nature of relationships, normative beliefs, and the ways in which things get done (Brown & Rodriguez, 2009, p. 224).

Thus, school culture is where meaning is made, identities are forged, and truth is coconstructed. The research has demonstrated that school culture helps provide a more complex understanding of the role that schools play in shaping students' experiences, and has been shown to directly impact student success and failure (Conchas, 2001; Rodriguez, 2005; Rodriguez, 2008; Valenzuela, 1999). School culture is also the point at which individuals in a school setting are able to interact with, respond to, and transform school policy, curriculum, and procedures. Similarly, school culture is the intersection between the impact of policy and its effect on individual agency, such as the dispositions, behaviors, and perspectives and experiences that students have in school (see Figure 2.1). Thus, school culture allows itself to be unveiled when epistemological and methodological frameworks, such as PUEDES, are available for stakeholders to acknowledge, examine, and create.

PUEDES Brings Complexity

In addition to the operationalization of the different concepts, it is important to recognize how the PUEDES approach provides a three-dimensional method of understanding why students drop out or are pushed out of school. Such an approach promotes an inclusive consideration of the ways that school policy, student-adult relationships, and individual student motivation, for example, provide a much more comprehensive explanation of the dropout problem. Such complexity is necessary when many perspectives, especially from a deficit-oriented paradigm, tend to blame students, their culture, or their families for their academic failure (see Valencia, 1997 for a critique of the deficit approach). Rather, the interactive nature of PUEDES encourages one to consider at least three perspectives and the ways in which they interact and intersect with one another.

For instance, the dominant narrative in schools and society would have us believe that students drop out because of their own wrongdoing. Such a perspective tends to isolate the problem as an issue of agency, not educational policy or factors associated with school culture such as the quality of student-adult connections and relationships in school (Valenzuela, 1999). Such a depiction of the problem is shortsighted and too simplistic. Framing dropout as such also allows a policy maker, teacher, principal, counselor, or any other school stakeholder to absolve him or herself from the problem, or isolate the problem within the individual, not the environment, and in this case, school environment. If you follow that logic, the implications for framing the problem in such a way have far-reaching consequences for determining how to respond to the dropout crisis (Brown & Rodriguez, 2009). If agency is framed as static, such as one's disposition toward school (i.e., student does not like school), then the solution is created around the individual. So, if we learn that a student finds school boring, then the student is identified as someone who "lacks interest." But PUEDES helps implicate how a student's boredom is actually quite dynamic when understood within the context of the curriculum (structure) offered in school and the quality of teaching and relationships that this student has or does not have with school adults or peers, for that matter (culture). In this case, we move from a simplistic and deficit analysis to an explanation that is likely to be much more complex. The PUEDES approach is represented in Figure 2.2, and captures how a student's boredom is likely to be influenced by irrelevant curriculum and detached relationships with school adults, for example.

Figure 2.2. The PUEDES Approach

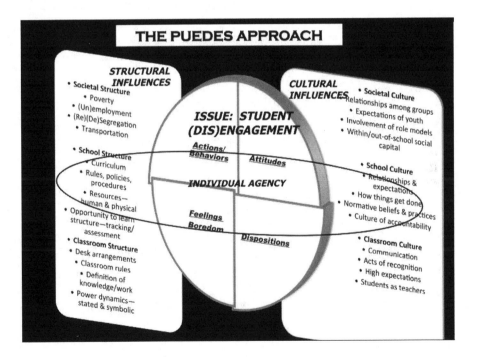

PUEDES Recognizes Power

The original framework proposed by Datnow et al. (2002) visually positioned structure, culture, and agency in a seemingly equal way. That is, while structure, culture, and agency are powerful analytical perspectives alone and interactive in nature, as conceptualized by Datnow et al. (2002), there needs to be a power analysis between structure and agency, structure and culture, culture and agency, and all three in relation to one another. The application of the framework to an actual situation (see Ramon's experience, below) suggests that there indeed is a power differential among the different dimensions, especially if a student (in the case of low-income students of color) is in a relatively powerless position in relation to the institution (i.e., school). While power varies by position within any given institution (i.e., school, family, job, university, etc.), PUEDES helps illuminate how the various structures and processes within school shape student agency. For instance, while a ninth-grade Latino student may know that attending school and aiming for high grades is important, dropping out of school may result in irreparable damages to the student, his or her family, future earnings, health, and general quality-of-life indicators. Research also shows that dropping out of school increases one's reliance on the social-services system (i.e., welfare, incarceration, unemployment). However, when a student drops out, the institution (school) by and large remains the same. The policies, procedures, and rules do not change, and relationships, belief systems, and institutional practices remain unaltered. Thus, while dimensions of structure, culture, and agency all do play a role in explaining why a student succeeds or fails in school, there are power imbalances that need to be acknowledged and analyzed in order to fully understand the complexity of dropout and/or pushout. The PUEDES approach brings this analytical perspective to the conversation, and suggests that power indeed matters and needs to be acknowledged when understanding and responding to the dropout crisis.

Using the PUEDES Approach to Shape Equitable Responses

The application of PUEDES is not only useful for analytical purposes, but it is also useful in designing implications for policy, practice, and future research on the topic. For instance, in the case of the bored student above, a narrow-minded solution might attempt to somehow fix the student's boredom by telling him that school is important and that he should take interest. The student might even be referred to a guidance counselor so that he can be convinced that he should take interest in school because an education is important for one's future. However, the PUEDES approach facilitates opportunities for a school principal, for instance, to reflect on the landscape of the school, and examine how the structure of the school, such as the size, the curriculum, or the way time is structured in the class, may be contributing to student boredom. The principal may even learn from the student experience by visiting classrooms or shadowing the student for a day to see how he or she experiences boredom. This type of exercise is a potentially powerful learning experience that can benefit student engagement, and an opportunity for school leadership to examine what is successful and what needs to be improved in the school. Similarly, a consideration of school culture may encourage a principal to see how expectations are relayed to students, view how students and teachers interact with one another, evaluate the degree to which the pedagogical experiences in the classroom are engaging and interesting, or even witness the extent to which dialoguing and the coconstruction of knowledge and meaning is encouraged or not. All together, the PUEDES approach contextualizes student boredom, as an initial signal of individual agency, within the school context that helps us understand that boredom or engagement is coconstructed by factors and processes associated with the agency of the student *and* the structure and culture of the school.

In the case of Black and Latina/o students who graduate at rates around 50%, the PUEDES approach is particularly timely as the nation continues to struggle with the test-centered culture triggered by No Child Left Behind over a decade ago and hardly altered by Race to the Top. In this context, the PUEDES approach seems to be all the more necessary to help facilitate equity-minded research, policy, and practices related to Black and Latina/o and other marginalized youth. To illuminate the analytical significance of PUEDES, Ramon's story is discussed below.

Ramon

Ramon was a research participant in a mixed-methods research study examining student-centered perspectives on school structure, culture, and achievement in a large, urban school district in the Northeast. Ramon's story evolved out of this larger study, and subsequently dropped out during data collection. Interestingly, and upon reflection on the larger project, Ramon was not one of the initially selected participants; rather, he learned about the project through a friend, and expressed interest in participating when he found out that we were trying to learn about the student experience. It seemed as if Ramon was looking for an outlet to share his experience and insight, and our project was a perfect outlet.

When the project began, Ramon was a 17-year-old, Latino, tenth grader. He lived in a single-parent home and attended Grand High School (GHS), a large, comprehensive school serving a low-income, racially diverse student population—about half Latina/o and half Black and/or African American. GHS and its larger community reflect the demographic realities of large, urban centers across the country—majority-minority, majority low-income students, and significant numbers of English Learner students. GHS was selected as a research site because of its recent reform initiatives and for its pervasive struggle to escape a history of academic failure.

Contrary to much of the quantitative research that paints a profile of invisibility and isolationism of the typical school dropout, Ramon was an academically stellar and socially engaged student known by most adults and students. He attended a highly competitive, public middle school but withdrew for reasons associated with what he called "cultural alienation." He had a savvy street intellect that allowed him to successfully navigate the urban terrain, and shared examples of how such experiences were denied or made unwelcome in the classroom. By the 10th grade, he successfully passed the math and reading portions of the state's high school exit exams, and was poised, at least on paper, to graduate from high school.

Interestingly, the dominant narrative explaining why he dropped out of school would suggest that he was unmotivated to excel, incapable of completing the academic work, and was likely to be socially and academically detached and disengaged from school. But an application of the PUEDES approach provides an opportunity to engage in a much more complex understanding of how the coconstruction of school structure, culture, and agency contributed to Ramon's disengagement with and eventual departure from school, or in other words, how he was pushed out of school.

Methodology

The data for this study was collected over the course of one academic year. Three in-depth interviews were conducted with Ramon, in which he described various aspects of his schooling experiences, such as his relationships with school adults and peers, his experiences and perspectives about school rules and practices, and his thoughts and experiences toward learning. All of the interviews were recorded and transcribed verbatim. In addition to the interviews, I also observed Ramon for at least 50 hours by "shadowing" him in school to get a sense of his everyday experiences. During some of these observations, I engaged in informal discussions with Ramon. From these observations and discussions, detailed field notes were typed (Emerson, Fretz, & Shaw, 1995). Interview transcripts and field notes were uploaded into ATLASti, a qualitative data-analysis software package, in which the data was coded. Coding was largely inductive; that is, I focused primarily on what was significant to Ramon (Miles & Huberman, 1994). Cross-case and cross-theme comparisons were performed within and across interviews and observations to understand the complexity of Ramon's engagement and disengagement from school (Maxwell & Miller, 1991).

Applying PUEDES to Ramon's Situation

Data from interviews and observations with Ramon portrayed him as a critical, disengaged, neglected, socially and intellectually alienated, yet socially engaged, inquisitive, and critically conscious individual. A superficial analysis would bring one to the conclusion that Ramon lacked interest in the academic content, complained too much about school, and when possible, skipped class and slyly defied authority. However, a deeper and more complex analysis demonstrated an interaction of school-based structural and cultural processes that shaped his individual agency, which only denied him opportunities to engage with school.

Ramon: How Structure, Culture, and Agency Pushed Him Out of School

Upon entry to the school, our research objective was clear—to learn from the experiences and perspectives of students, particularly in the context of several school-reform initiatives. One of the district reform efforts revolved around the implementation of schools-within-a school and theme-based small learning communities. In the middle of the reform effort, Ramon critiqued the small learning community effort by connecting it to a critique of the curriculum and resource availability (i.e., books):

> The school's not challenging... [Besides] All we learn about is Christopher Columbus but most kids don't know what really happened. We need new books and keep them up to date—recycle the old books. Sincerely, school is bullshit. I thought there were going to be opportunities, like in Arts Applications [a small learning community] but it is not happening. In World Relations [small learning community] they are learning about [city's name]. We already learned about [city's name] in the 2nd grade. Why are we still learning it? (Ramon's Interview)

During my interviews with Ramon, he mentioned, on more than one occasion, the issue of curricular repetition. For Ramon, these structures were insulting, irrelevant, and failed to meet his expectations as a student. Later, Ramon critiqued the implementation of the small learning communities by linking it to a worsened social and/or interpersonal environment between students and teachers. This socially alienating environment, according to Ramon, also contributed to a culture of "nobody cares" for students:

> The only change I see [after small learning communities] is that the adults don't know you... There is no sense of community—nobody cares [about school] except the teachers. School is like a popularity contest—they [students] don't care about learning. The schools asks, "what [small learning community] do you want to be in?" not, "what do you want to learn?" I am in Art Applications and they are not teaching anything related to that. (Ramon's Interview)

Ramon identified a key contradiction between the school's zero-tolerance late policy (structure) and what actually happened to students once they were inside the building. For Ramon, there was too much concentration and control over student movement and location versus whether they were engaged and learning (culture). When asked about his general feelings toward school, it was apparent that the school's discipline policy as a school structure was unfair, and had unintended consequences. For Ramon, pushing students away was another indication that there was little accountability for the presence or well-being of students:

> I feel that it [school] is a waste of time sometimes. Half of the time you aren't learning. About 1/2 of the people don't want to learn, about 15 out of 30. I don't like it [school]. I want to take GED and go to community college. They [school] have this stupid late policy that if you are late after 7:55 a.m. This is bad because they send students away, push them off. I am not a little boy, I shouldn't have to have my mom with me [when I come late to school]. It [discipline policy] has no purpose to deal with things in life. [Besides] Punishment is a vacation. Most kids know the consequences and usually get suspended on Thursday or Friday for a 5-day weekend. Then there is detention but some students have jobs. You just sit there for an hour after school. (Ramon's Interview)

"Not learning anything" was a frequent theme for Ramon and many of the students who were interviewed for the project. Lacking interest would not be an apt descriptor for Ramon, as he had interest and thoughtful, critical commentary about September 11, 2001, and the wars in the Middle East.

In addition to the apparent structure-culture contradictions illuminated by Ramon's critiques, he also believed that the school's mistreatment of Latina/o students (culture) was in part attributed to teachers and the school:

> Spanish kids [Latinas/os] have the most trouble [in school]. Nobody motivates them here [at school]…ou have to motivate them from early on—you can't just begin at 17 years old. You have to begin when they are small. The problem is not with the students, it's with the school. (Ramon's Interview)

Motivation, according to Ramon, had to be directly addressed in order to respond to the needs of Latina/o students. Upon analysis, Ramon could have been projecting his own experiences to those of his peers suggesting that he needed more adult intervention to motivate him. And, while friendly and cordial with most of the school adults, he believed the solution lay with the presence of strong teachers:

> [A good teacher is] A teacher that can relate to her students—teachers are usually authoritarian—no one wants that—but a teacher who sees you like a friend—who is

down with me—students like that. For example, Mr. Carter, he respects us, we respect him. You can't gain respect by demand—you have to earn it by respecting.
Ms. Kendall is cool—she respects kids—they will do the work. There is a difference
between a good person and a bad teacher. Do they know what they are teaching?
Some teachers don't know what they are teaching. Some need the teacher's guide-
book. (Ramon's Interview)

It is important to note that Ramon dichotomized teachers as two potentially separate beings—those who are good teachers, and those who are bad
teachers but good people. This insight speaks to his thirst for strong, intellectual engagement, even in the presence of decent interpersonal connections
(culture) with school adults. In other words, for Ramon, he had amicable, respectful, and in some cases, asymmetrical, power struggles and relationships
with his teachers; however these connections did not automatically translate
to the rich academic engagement for which he seemed to yearn.

Ramon's experiences were not simply detailed in our one-on-one interviews. I also conducted hours of ethnographic observations as I shadowed
Ramon from class to class, during lunch, and after school. One repetitive cultural theme within the classroom was the absence of instruction, as reflected
in Ramon's notion of "not learning anything." To capture the complex and
coconstructive nature of Ramon's disposition and disengagement from
school as a function of the structure, culture, and his own agency, here is an
excerpt from an observation:

I pulled Ramon from first period. Before we left to the cafeteria, Mr. Dixon asked
Ramon if he had completed his assignments and Ramon said that all he had to do
was print them out. Mr. Dixon requested that he print them out before we leave and
Ramon did so. As we walked to the cafeteria, I asked Ramon what the assignment
was about and Ramon said that they had to answer a question in paragraph form,
import a picture from the web and print it out. It seemed mundane and resonates
with Ramon's previous contentions that, "'they' (the teachers/the school) really
don't teach us anything." (Field notes)

Upon reflection, Ramon was wrong in one of his assertions. He was indeed learning something. He was learning that it was acceptable to attend
school, get hassled if not in school on time, and in some cases get turned
away, then encouraged to go to class, yet find oneself in an environment that
did not engage students in any meaningful or intellectual, rich discussions.

It seemed that over time, Ramon's experiences with the structural and
cultural environment of the school and classroom life fueled his agency to
critique school. Perhaps due to the lack of dialogical spaces to discuss school
or other critical issues about which he had much to say, he consoled with
peers, and occasionally talked with teachers and sometimes the researcher

during an interview or observations. This ongoing critique seemed to further alienate and marginalize him, likely because no one really had a response to his critique of what was happening.

Ramon's experiences with the school's discipline policies and curriculum (structure), and his sense of "not learning anything" and that there was an issue with apathetic teachers (culture) who did not take responsibility for motivating Latina/o students triggered his outward discontent with school and schooling (agency). His discontent seemed to trigger a subtle yet symbolic marginalization by school adults, particularly when his critiques were directly and indirectly aimed at them. The PUEDES framework demonstrates that the coconstruction of Ramon's experiences is much more complex than any thoughtless critique of him "not caring about school." PUEDES helps explain how Ramon's decision to eventually leave school and drop out (agency) was actually shaped by various structural and cultural factors and processes in school.

Understanding Ramon's Situation Through the PUEDES Approach

Ramon undoubtedly valued education. He was unquestionably intelligent, insightful, and had excellent interpersonal skills. While he spoke eagerly about a wealth of issues, he failed to find a responsive structure or cultural environment within the school that could commiserate with him, or through which he could engage in dialogue. In isolation, one may conclude that the small learning community structure failed to benefit students like Ramon, or that the low expectations for Latina/o students as part of the school's culture contributed to Ramon's isolation and disengagement. However, it was the process of schooling all together that contributed to the coconstruction of Ramon's critique and disengagement from school. In other words, it was not just one factor or process that contributed to his ultimate departure from school; rather, it was a combination of structural, cultural, and individual agency.

Specifically, Ramon's experiences and perspectives show a complex interplay between the various factors associated with societal, school, and classroom structure; with societal, school, and classroom culture; and Ramon's agency. In Figure 2.3 the spiral rings show the interconnected relationship between structure, agency, and culture. For instance, PUEDES allows us to recognize that poverty (structure) shapes student (dis)engagement (agency), as does communication and expectations (culture) within the culture of the classroom. Similarly, disengagement from school (agency) is also a function of one's relationships with school adults (culture) and the extent to which students are given a voice in school (structure). Further, individual critiques of schooling (agency) may very well be shaped by the power dynamics between students and adults within the school environment (structure) that are likely to influence the ways in which students and adults interact or fail to interact in the larger community (culture). The spirals imply that the three factors are reflective, in that structure influences culture as culture influences structure, structure influences agency as agency influences structure, and culture influences agency as agency influences culture. Thus, rather than focusing solely on one reason why students like Ramon drop out or are pushed out (i.e., the fact that he felt school was a "waste of time"), the PUEDES framework not only allows for a consideration of multiple factors, but the interplay of those factors. Let us take a closer look at Ramon's situation using PUEDES as an analytical framework (Figure 2.4).

Figure 2.3. Ramon's Agency

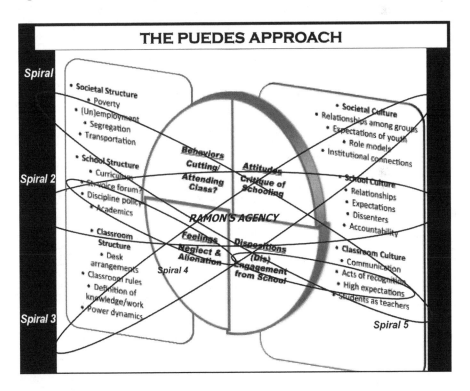

For instance, Spiral 1 in Figure 2.3 shows how Ramon's inability to access challenging and relevant curriculum (structure), in conjunction with Ramon's interpretation of low expectations for Latina/o students (culture), helped shape his negative critique of school (agency). On a related issue, Spiral 2 refers to how Ramon's critique of school further pushed some teachers away (culture)

and even contributed to a climate of weak accountability for students like Ramon (culture), which may have made the small learning community efforts (structure) seem ineffective and the curriculum uninteresting (structure).

Ramon also found that his desire to dialogue and engage (agency) in debate was subtracted by an irrelevant curriculum (structure) and through the adults' inability to challenge him (culture), as demonstrated by Spiral 3 in Figure 2.3. Thus, the school's weak accountability for student learning (culture), in part as a function of the institutional power of adults through the enforcement of the school's discipline policy (structure), operated to create a climate that silenced dissenters like Ramon (culture), and that gradually pushed Ramon away from school (agency), as suggested by Spiral 4 in Figure 2.3.

Ramon experienced a culture of dismissiveness that signaled to him that no one cared and therefore there was no accountability for student learning or well-being (culture). Over time, Ramon increasingly questioned the viability of his own role as a student, in the face of teachers' failure to nurture and respect him as an intellectual being (agency). That is, while Ramon was clearly a visible presence in school, as evident through his popularity with school adults, the same adults also rendered him invisible by denying his intellectual thirst for engagement with school. Ramon's visible invisibility speaks to the need for schools to recognize the intellectual, relational, and personal dimensions to students' existence in school (see Rodriguez, 2012 for a theoretical discussion of a Praxis of Recognition).

Nonetheless, it is imperative to recognize the asymmetrical power dynamic between institutional structure and culture versus individual student agency. That is, while Ramon expressed his discontent with school (agency), it was the relational dynamics between Ramon and school adults (culture), compounded by the school's policies and procedures (structure) that determined how the institution responded to his dissent. In other words, dissent alone did not equal his exportation from school, but worked in tandem with the rules, policies, and procedures (structures) in operation at his school, along with the culture of accountability and receptivity to or deflection of students like Ramon who are obviously unhappy with the realities of school life (culture). This suggests that schools, as institutions of power over the marginalized students, must recognize this power imbalance, and work to respond and not punish and marginalize students like Ramon. The graphic representation of PUEDES attempts to visually depict how the overbearing and sometimes overpowering nature of the "Structural Influences" are positioned in relation to Individual Agency and Cultural Influences.

Next Steps: Putting PUEDES Into Action

Ramon's experiences are unfortunately all too common among low-income and working-class Black and Latina/o youth and other youth of color across the country. PUEDES suggests that the interplay between the policy and curricular environment, along with Ramon's progressive disengagement, was facilitated by a cultural environment of low academic expectations, the silencing of dissent, lack of adult caring, and a general culture of apathy toward Ramon's detachment from school. In-depth ethnographic studies have confirmed the prevalence of these conditions serving low-income youth of color, especially Black and Latina/o students (Lopez, 2003; Nieto, 1999; Valenzuela, 1999).

Nevertheless, there needs to be an honest conversation about what schools can and cannot do. We cannot expect schools to remedy all these matters, especially when youth at risk of dropping out are facing social and economic challenges beyond the limits of what schools can provide (Noguera, 2003). Schools alone cannot eradicate poverty. Schools alone cannot create or find jobs for parents. Schools alone cannot promise access to quality health care. Schools alone cannot guarantee that children and youth will eat breakfast before school or dinner after school, nor can they ensure decent and safe housing. However, there are several things schools *can do* to help reduce the dropout crisis and promote engagement, achievement, and improved graduation rates, especially among low-income youth of color in our public schools.

In order to move forward, we need bold policies and practices that contribute to an environment where students like Ramon can thrive. As mentioned, the PUEDES approach can be utilized as a guide that proposes policy and practical responses through a structure, culture, and agency perspective. The following recommendations are based on the premise that grassroots change must be instituted from the level of the people—in this case, school adults and young people, alongside parents, courageous policy makers, and the community (Freire, 1973a, 1973b; Noguera, 2003; Rodriguez & Brown, 2009). That is, in order for any of these recommendations to succeed, there needs to be cross-institutional collaboration, shared accountability, and a focus on process *and* outcome. Below is a set of recommendations that emanate directly from the PUEDES approach, and focus on the cultural influences at the school level that help shape student engagement.

Using the PUEDES Approach to Boost Student Engagement and Achievement

If the end goal is to promote student engagement, reduce dropout, and orchestrate student achievement and success, we must insist that school structure, school culture, and student agency be considered together. Using the PUEDES approach, I will discuss how student engagement can be improved and enhanced when certain cultural elements within schools work in conjunction with school structure and individual agency. For the purposes of this chapter, I will focus on three cultural elements:

(1) Engaging youth as intellectuals,
(2) Listening to marginalized students, and
(3) Investing in relationships

Figure 2.4 is a replica of the original framework, but focuses on various structural and cultural responses that can shape individual agency and enhance a culture that boosts student engagement and achievement. In Figure 2.4, the spiral is deliberately wider than previously characterized. The purpose of the wider spiral insinuates that establishing a relationship-rich culture that values each member of the community, and positions youth as intellectuals, will result in a culture that is much more likely to engage students meaningfully and equitably.

Figure 2.4. Toward Equitable Schools and Outcomes

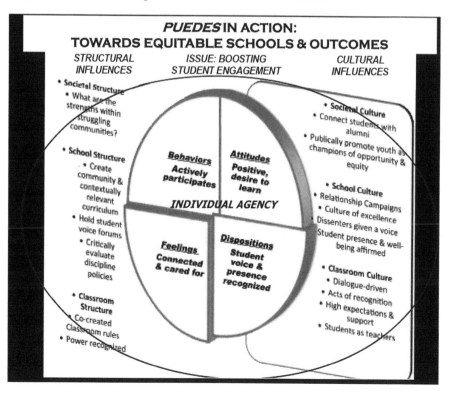

Engaging youth as intellectuals.

The role of youth in the process of educational change has been the topic of inquiry over the last decade, particularly using Participatory Action Research (PAR) (Cammarota & Fine, 2008; Cammarota & Romero, 2009; Rodriguez & Brown, 2009). In PAR-related projects, the role of youth shifts from objects to active subjects within the research process (Rodriguez & Brown, 2009). In such initiatives, youth are encouraged to raise their consciousness about the world in which they live (Freire, 1973a, 1973b). Through the research process, participants also learn about identifying and framing issues and problems in their schools and communities, creating research questions and design, learning data analysis, and producing a final presentation to be shared with relevant stakeholders. Equally important is learning to question and dialogue (Solorzano, 1989). Through PAR-related initiatives, youth begin to recognize their role as critical, intellectual actors, especially in an environment such as the school where such practices should be the norm. Stakeholders need to create opportunities (structures) for youth to share their knowledge, become the teacher, and coconstruct meaning (agency), when the environment is safe and receptive (culture). When such opportunities are available, youth can frame themselves as public intellectuals, as they begin to transform their identities as actors within the process of positive social and educational change (Rodriguez & Brown, 2009). From this perspective, students are not mere recipients of knowledge; rather, they are active constructors of knowledge and knowledge-sharing. The positionality of youth shifts from students to champions of equity and opportunity within their schools and in their communities.

To facilitate this process, educators can work directly with youth to develop curricular and pedagogical activities that treat the classroom, school, and community as a social laboratory. If students gripe about irrelevant curriculum, unfair school or community policies, or low expectations, these experiences become topic areas for research inquiry. Teachers must be willing to explore, question, and adjust as the project unfolds. Teachers must have the support of local leadership, and local leadership needs to be courageous enough to listen and lead their faculty into dialogue with youth. Equally important is the role of community. Because the youth can and should be sharing much of their work publicly, teachers and school leadership must ensure that students are supported by key allies such as parents, school alumni, and key community actors who will support their research and suggestions for policy and practice.

In turn, promoting youth as intellectuals challenges and even incorporates curricular structures, indirectly establishes a stage for student voice, and can even implicate some of the school's policies. In the process, and as a result of this type of student engagement, students exercise their individual agency through active participation, demonstrating a desire to learn and engage. They are likely to feel connected and as though they belong to a community of caring adults, and feel recognized as human beings because someone is listening and legitimizing their experiences. PUEDES serves as a guide to help forward-thinking reformers understand and transform the educational space to engage students.

Listening to marginalized students.

Another way the PUEDES approach serves as a tool for designing equitable responses to the dropout crisis is to focus on historically marginalized students. It is widely believed that motivated, involved, and achieving students are typically the most engaged students in school. Because of previous academic preparation, involvement in special programs (i.e., college-prep programs such as AVID), and enrollment in highly selective courses, students essentially assume the identity—either through their own identification or that of the school and/or teachers—of young people on a pathway toward academic and personal success. These students are likely to be involved in school activities such as student council. By and large school is working for them, they cause minimal disruption in school, and administration and teachers may even use them as examples of how the school is actually working well for students.

But what about quiet students or those that are silenced by policies, practices, and processes in school? What about the students who are not engaged with school, not involved in activities, and not taking the most selective classes? What about the students who are critical of school, and sometimes find themselves on a path of removal by school processes and practices (Brown & Rodriguez, 2009; Fine, 1987). Sometimes, these students may even be those that are acting out in class, giving teachers a hard time, and have sparse attendance. Some of my own research shows that these students can often be the most insightful about solutions for school improvement and promoting student engagement (Brown & Rodriguez, 2009; Rodriguez & Wasserberg, 2010).

Concerns, experiences, and the expertise of students like Ramon typically go unregistered, and thus their voices and experiences are silenced. Yet, when given the opportunity to share, reflect, and critique the school, they tend to provide great insight into the inner workings of school life, and provide perspectives that can inform the work of teachers, school leadership, and policy makers. Stakeholders should seek out and centralize the voices and experiences of these students as a mechanism to promote a school culture that is reflective and deliberate in producing student success.

One way to establish this culture is to identify the spaces these students are most likely to occupy. These spaces can be a particular table at lunch, in-house suspension, or in the vice-principal's office awaiting disciplinary action. These kinds of spaces need to be deliberately created and consistent over a period of time. These efforts can be framed as "learning from student" forums or focus groups. Those who carry out these efforts will learn that students are honest and quite forthcoming about their experiences and about what works and does not work in school. Students also will be honest and sometimes even protective about the information they wish to disclose, particularly when it involves certain teachers. These moments are vitally important for understanding the investment these students have in the school. Imagine what it means when a seemingly disengaged student goes out of his or her way to protect the identity of mediocre or weak teachers. Similarly, what does it mean when a student is completely forthright in their willingness to put a teacher "on blast" who is doing a disservice to students and the school. In either case, these students need to be protected and heard.

Observers will notice that committing to and establishing a culture of listening to the marginalized student voice not only pushes the boundaries on capitalizing on existing school structures (i.e., in-house suspension), but it also shapes individual student agency by perhaps shifting the way students engage with school. By feeling that someone is listening, they may feel more connected to particular adults and to school. They may begin to shift their distant relationship with school to one that may be more optimistic and engaged. Further, and perhaps most importantly, marginalized students may begin to feel that their experiences and stories are legitimized and that their presence is valued. Feeling like someone is paying attention can be the catalyst for facilitating student connectedness and engagement. Again, PUEDES acts not only as an analytical tool but as a resource to envision and implement equity-driven policies and practices that aim to engage students.

Investing in relationships.

At least 15 years of solid research shows that student-adult relationships in schools matter, especially for Latina/o and Black youth across the United States (I will revisit all three recommendations in the 10-Point Plan in Chapter 4). Like Ramon, many youth are eager to find adults who are "down" with them, who are committed, and respectful. For too long, educational policy such as NCLB has created a narrow definition of a qualified teacher. For youth of color, a college degree, a credential, and knowledge of subject area are not enough. Schools serving low-income youth and youth of color need teachers who recognize, inspire, motivate, and support their students. School leaders should find evidence of these kinds of practices and characteristics when hiring and evaluating teachers. Educators who do this need to be recognized and applauded, and those that fall short need to "reinvent" themselves, as encouraged by the work of Paulo Freire. Furthermore, the research is clear; relationships are a reflection of school culture, and are often the gateway to student engagement and learning (Rodriguez, 2003).

In order to emphasize the critical role that relationships play in boosting student engagement with school, there is a need for school and community campaigns that focus on relationships. School leadership, teachers, and students need to dialogue about the significance of relationships in people's lives and in the context of learning. A committee should be developed that recognizes those who believe in and invest in relationship-building in school. Community members should investigate the nuances of relationships, how they are formed, how they are sustained, and how they are used to boost student engagement and achievement. Relationships are perhaps the most inexpensive solution to the problem of vast inequity across most low-income school systems in the United States.

A relationship-rich culture not only begs questions of structure, such as traditional power dynamics between students and adults, or negotiating school rules, but relationships are likely to shape student participation, introduce opportunities for students, boost student connectedness, and affirm student presence in school. This culture in turn shapes other cultural dimensions of school life such as high expectations, student support, and multiple forms of recognition (Rodriguez, 2012).

The PUEDES approach moves us away from the long-standing assumption that a student's success or failure is solely a matter of individual agency. Such a perspective is too simple and shortsighted. The PUEDES approach aims to push our understanding, analysis, and response to bolder and more relevant levels. Until our analysis is transformed into large-scale policy and practice, we are likely to go another 20 years without any significant progress.

In the interim, we must push forward. The next chapter provides an overview of three initiatives that take the lessons learned and insights gleaned from the PUEDES approach and apply them to a series of action research activities that engage students, teachers, community stakeholders, and policy makers to respond to the dropout crisis.

CHAPTER THREE

Institutional Culture Under the Spotlight: Black and Latina/o Students' Voices and Experiences in Three Urban Cities

Discovering Recognition and Centering Student Voice

My dissertation research at Harvard was a rather conventional, mixed-methods study on the relationship between school structure and culture and their effects on academic achievement across three significantly different high schools in the Boston area. My study was a smaller project that evolved from a larger study involving 10 high schools across Boston and other nearby cities led by Dr. Pedro Noguera. As the lead research assistant on the project, I was particularly concerned with the role that "personalization" played in the lived experiences of primarily low-income Black and Latina/o students (Conchas & Rodriguez, 2007; Rodriguez, 2005; Rodriguez, 2008). I used personalization as a conceptual lens, because many of the reform efforts around small learning communities espoused a more personalized experience for students; yet I was intrigued by what that meant in a racially diverse city plagued by poverty and segregation for generations. I was also committed to listening to and learning from the voices and experiences of students themselves—a group that has historically been excluded from educational research, especially low-income students of color (Nieto, 1999).

As I conducted interviews and engaged in ethnographic observations of everyday school life for nearly two years, I began to dig into the nuances of personalization from the perspective of students. I examined how "knowing," "talking," "pushing," and "respecting" were vital elements to personalization (Rodriguez, 2003). Students believed that relationships were critical to their connectedness with school, and an absence of these relationships often resulted in tenuous and what later evolved into politicized analyses of relationships (Valenzuela, 1999). What was particularly profound about my observations revolved around the passivity associated with the presence or absence of personalization. Most of the literature discussed personalization as something that "happens to" students. In other words, they are either personalized or not. What was missing from the literature, but what was glaringly obvious from my ethnographic fieldwork, was that personalization was something that people practiced, avoided, or ignored. And, it became in-

creasingly apparent over time that relationships, as an indicator of personalization, were in fact a make-or-break deal for many students who struggled
to see relevance and meaning in school, such as Ramon (whose experiences
were discussed in depth in Chapter 2). That is, not only was the curriculum
often detached from and irrelevant to their everyday realities in a complex
social, political, economic, and historical environment, but the people that
attempted to "teach" them were often unable or unwilling to engage them in
a personally meaningful way.

These observations led to a series of thought exercises and theoretical
explorations to help make sense of what the students were experiencing and
what I was trying to make sense of in real time. I knew that I was in a privileged position as a Harvard graduate student conducting research in a high-
poverty community that was technically not my own. Yet, my transplant
status from southern California to urban Boston provided certain leveraging
points, and afforded me insider access that allowed me to navigate and connect with the community that eventually became my own. For me, my research became increasingly political, and I knew that my evolution as a
researcher and advocate for the historically silenced was being cemented as I
continued on with my journey through the dissertation process. Simultaneously, I was engaging in a series of reflections back to my own educational
experiences as a public school student in Southern California, and engaging
in some deep, intellectual engagement as I read some of the godmothers and
fathers of critical theory and pedagogy, led by one of my mentors at Harvard,
Dr. Eileen de los Reyes.

One of the assignments that I completed for her class while I was collecting my dissertation data in the field was around the investigation of a concept. We were delving deeply into colonization by Albert Memmi, violence
by Frantz Fanon, war of position by Antonio Gramsci, critical consciousness
by Paulo Freire, power-within by Starhawk, teaching to transgress by bell
hooks, and many others. I was intrigued by Freire's notion of critical consciousness and what role that played in school life. I began to ask about the
conditions that needed to be in place that contributed to the development of
critical consciousness among students. I also began to look at historical cases
of student resistance against and engagement with the political system, particularly the Chicano Student Walkouts in East Los Angeles in 1968. As I
was collecting my data, reading about consciousness, and delving deeply into
the 1968 Blowouts, I began to explore the role that recognition (not personalization) played in the development of critical consciousness. It seemed to me
that in order for one to develop that critical consciousness, particularly in
school or any educational setting, there needed to be a dialogical encounter

between oneself and the other. In the context of my data collection, I began to think about the presence of recognition, not only as an active and deliberate practice, but the complex nature of recognition between students and adults, particularly through an analysis of power. This was significant, because it seemed that school adults had a fair degree of autonomy when relating to or reaching out to students. Some students had strong connections, some did not, and many others were symbolically invisible.

As I continued with data collection for my dissertation, I grew increasingly appreciative of the role students' voices and experiences played in teaching researchers, teachers, school leaders, and policymakers about the realities of school life. I heard painful narratives of disrespect, embarrassment, and dehumanization in the classroom. I heard the ills of misguided and misdirected school policy. I heard about the repetitive nature of curriculum. And above all, I heard about the inconsequential nature of their presence and how this was affirmed by the lack of relationships, largely irrelevant curriculum, and oppressive educational policies.

What began as a purely relational analysis of recognition eventually evolved into a consideration of recognition through the lenses of curriculum, pedagogy, the context of students' lives, and the purpose of education (Rodriguez, 2012). This developing framework began to inform a related but new direction of my research: the student as an *agent* of research and transformation, versus the student as *subject* of research and change (Rodriguez & Brown, 2009). These experiences sparked a parallel project that sought to do just that.

Boston: The PROS Project

While there has been considerable work on the role that students' voices can play in informing education reform and change, I was fortunate enough to engage in a project that repositioned students from simple data points as informants to researchers, to active agents of change as participant-researchers (Rodriguez & Brown, 2009). One of my colleagues wrote a mini-grant to a local foundation that funded projects around student engagement issues. Given our findings from the larger project led by Dr. Pedro Noguera, a few of us began a parallel journey over an 18-month period that would engage students in a series of problem-posing pedagogies (Freire, 1973b) that evolved into a Participatory Action Research (PAR) project in 2003.

Our small research team approached one of the lowest performing high schools in Boston and sought out a partnership. The principal immediately identified a young and dynamic English teacher that could partner with us to examine educational issues most relevant to students. After a series of brainstorming sessions led by the question, "Why do students drop out of school," students identified several issues. They enthusiastically identified a laundry list of trouble issues in schools. After a few sessions, the teacher stated, "some students are talking and participating that I had no idea had so much to say about what's going on." We were convinced that Freire's problem-posing approach was indeed a trigger for rich dialogue and an engine to elicit generative themes produced by the students (Rodriguez, 2003).

One of the recurrent themes involved a "culture of low expectations." Students wanted to explore this issue in their school, so we guided them in a process to develop research questions, a methodology plan to collect and analyze data, timelines, and eventually a series of presentations back to the school—to students, teachers, and administration. Students interviewed and surveyed other students, teachers, counselors, and administrators. They found that students were guilty of holding low expectations of one another, while teachers perceived a culture of "not caring" which seemed to fuel their own disengagement from students. From this research, students opted to create a mini-documentary about their research, and eagerly sought multiple venues to share their findings with students, teachers, and administrators. In this project, the 20 students in the course became the researchers who then presented their research as seasoned public intellectuals to their communities. They developed a series of recommendations related to school policy and practice. We also invited several of the key research leaders to a panel at the Harvard Kennedy School of Government about educational reform and policy. As the facilitator, I wanted to ensure that youths' voices were at the table, so we stacked the panel with youth. One participant stated to the crowd, "Before the project, I was about to drop out and do hair. Now I am going to Northeastern University!" Alongside this project, our research team from the larger study held a series of youth forums led and organized by the youth. We invited our PROS group as a stakeholder group of youth. Students travelled to Harvard and engaged in a full-day activity on their idea of an ideal high school. Not only did students identify good lunches, small class size, and exciting opportunities in the classroom, but they also emphasized key culturally based factors and processes that contribute to school life, such as relationships, expectations, voice, and mutual respect between students and teachers.

The PROS project in Boston not only solidified my commitment to engaging students' voices to learn about the realities on the ground, but it also sparked a new level of engagement—providing youth with the opportunity to research, learn, and present research directly informed by their concerns, questions, and realities. The Participatory Action Research (PAR) process born in Boston followed me to Miami, where I launched a second project, The POWER Project.[1]

Miami: The POWER Project

When I arrived in Miami in the middle of 2005, I had just finished my graduate studies at Harvard and was eager to begin a new direction in my academic research and career. In 2006 I landed a tenure-track position at Florida International University (FIU), and soon became affiliated with the Center of Urban Education and Innovation in the College of Education led by renowned scholar, Dr. Lisa Delpit, and codirector, Dr. Joan Wynne. Given our overlapping interests, I learned about a series of challenges facing the city. When I arrived, I also learned that civil rights legend, Algebra Project founder, and MacArthur Award recipient, Bob Moses, also recently relocated to Miami to launch an Algebra Project initiative. As a Research Fellow with "The Center," I was just honored to be in the company of an incredible group of scholars committed to equity and social justice in our nation's schools and society.

Through the support of The Center, I identified the lowest performing school in the district, and what I later learned to be the lowest performing school in the state as well. This school earned a consecutive "F" rating year after year, faced pervasive leadership turnover, and was plagued by ongoing incidences of school violence. Located in downtown Miami in a historically impoverished community of Haitian and Latino immigrants, the school leadership identified a young, dynamic, and popular teacher that would eventually serve as our research partner. We quickly found common ground and shared similar philosophies about students and developing opportunities for engagement in school.

Because Miami-Dade County Public Schools had recently instituted a "zone" school-reform initiative, there were opportunities to see the effectiveness of this effort from the inside out and from the perspectives and experiences of students. However, we quickly learned that there were more significant challenges facing the school long before the implementation of the zone efforts (which involved longer school days, longer school years, more human and physical resources, among others). Students quickly shared narratives about the oppressive testing environment that swallowed every minute of school time—they spoke about test-prep English, test-prep Math,

---

1   The author would like to acknowledge the assistance of Dr. Martin Wasserberg, then Florida International University graduate student assistant, and now assistant professor at the University of North California-Wilmington.

then English, then Math, and then more practice tests. They also spoke about the impact of the FCAT, the Florida high-stakes testing system, on the social and cultural environment in school. Students felt silenced, they felt ignored, and they felt that there was no time for or attention to their social or relational needs. Curriculum was narrow and pedagogy suffered.

I later characterized this era as one of a *Test Prep Pedagogy* (Rodriguez, 2009). While the schools in Boston were at the mercy of state-wide, high-stakes testing as well, the ways in which the Florida schools, particularly the historically low-performing schools, responded to the new, state-wide mandates was quite distressing, particularly from the voices, experiences, and perspectives of students. This climate called for alternative pedagogies that were centered, once again, on student voice, critical thinking and engagement, and relationships. These familiar themes resonated with my findings from my dissertation and the PROS project in Boston. Thus, from these efforts, we launched the POWER project using Participatory Action Research (PAR) approaches so that the students could not only identify the challenges they were facing, but also play a direct role in devising a set of research-based recommendations and solutions (Cordova, 2004).

As with the PROS project in Boston, we used Freirean pedagogy by focusing on dialoguing, problem-posing approaches, and critical analysis (Freire, 1973). Over the course of a year and within the context of weekly classroom dialogues, we explored the realities, challenges, and experiences that were most familiar to the students' lives.

The Research and Relational Process: The POWER Project

Our research team included 20 Black and Latina/o 11th graders who volunteered to participate in the project that met for approximately seven hours a week for one academic year. The research team consisted of Martin Wasserberg, a graduate research assistant; the classroom teacher on record; the student researchers; and me, a university researcher. All classroom dialogue was used as ethnographic data, and pre/post individual interviews were conducted with all students.

One initial exercise centered on one question, "why do students dropout of school?" This dialogue snowballed into a laundry list of reasons including school and social/environmental reasons. Students mentioned testing, apathetic teachers, not having a voice, community violence, teen pregnancy, the need to work and support family, and health issues. This experience not only affirmed Freireian pedagogy with students who have historically been denied an opportunity to discuss these issues, but also demonstrated that students were more than ready to move forward and engage in a solution-driven effort to address some of the challenges they faced.

In addition to dialoguing, we focused on relationships (Rodriguez & Wasserberg, 2010). We not only aimed to practice "authentic" relationships (Valenzuela, 1999), but we also observed how students characterized and made sense of their everyday schooling experiences (Conchas & Rodriguez, 2007). We thought an emphasis on relationships was vital particularly in an urban context that has been historically structured to undermine relational and humanizing treatment (Kozol (2005).

Another integral characteristic of the project was our emphasis on group work and group process (this later informed The PRAXIS Project described below). We instituted a series of classroom routines such as a unity-clap and a "process-check" that encouraged students to reflect on their participation and that of others in the class. Students became noticeably conscious of themselves and others as we progressed over the year, particularly in the ways that they responded to other students' comments in class. We observed that prioritizing and establishing a classroom culture driven by norms and expectations around respect was vital to our success in the classroom.

Defining a "Qualified Teacher": The Students' Perspective

Similar to the PROS project in Boston, the students in The POWER Project engaged in a PAR project. The students decided that defining a "quality teacher" was one way to contribute to national conversation about school re-form and teacher quality. After a series of exercises and group projects, student-researchers defined good teachers as supportive, motivational, inspiring, respectful, and knew how to keep the classroom "alive." In small groups, students created 20-minute presentations, modeled these types of teachers, developed advice for current and future teachers, and made policy recommendations for K-12 and higher education. The culminating experience involved a presentation to pre-service teachers at Florida International University. In this case, not only did this university give the high school students an opportunity to visit campus for the first time, but it also allowed them to educate pre-service teachers about their definitions of a highly qualified teachers. In a sense, the student-researchers were delivering professional development to future teachers. The power dynamic shifted whereby the students became the teachers, educators, and intellectuals.

The Impact of The POWER Project

The experience of one student involved in the POWER project is illustrative of the impact such a project can have in our urban schools. In fact, Tina was

very similar to Ramon. She was very intelligent, critical, but had an underly-
ing distrust or uncertainty about what the school did versus what they advo-
cated.

For the first three months of the POWER project, we noticed Tina, who
sat in the back of the classroom and never participated in classroom discussions. Though present everyday and seemingly interested and engaged with
the dialogues through her body language and shaking of her head, she never
spoke. We had learned that she had been silenced, demeaned, and criticized
for being vocal in other classes in previous years, which led to her being cau-
tious and selective about engagement in our classroom dialogues. She had
been demeaned and criticized by many school adults in the past who claimed
to be there to help. Therefore, and understandably so, we had to prove our
dedication and earn her trust as community and school outsiders.

By the end of the year, Tina was a standout student. Her responses to re-
search-related discussions were often insightful, and manifested a deep understanding of the issues pertinent to her school and the community.
Specifically, Tina demonstrated a remarkable rapport with the adults and
students involved in the project in tackling the difficult dialogues around social-justice issues, equity, power, and privilege. She became a leader in the
classroom and of her small group project.

Inspired by her involvement and leadership on the project, she continued
working toward social-justice and equity issues throughout the summer and
into her senior year. With the help of our partner teacher and mentor to Tina,
she was appointed president of the city's Youth Council, and worked with
community adults to develop a curriculum to build bridges between students
and teachers across the city. In this role, she helped bring her high school
peers to college fairs and teen-leadership conferences, and her leadership
work earned her The Princeton Prize for the State of Florida, which recognizes a young person who addresses race relations in their work. She was
later flown to Princeton, where she met Professor Cornel West and received
her award. She later received a scholarship to a university in Florida.

The POWER project in Miami demonstrated that creating spaces for students to share their knowledge, expertise, and recommendations was vital to
their engagement in school. The question wasn't, "do our students have a
voice?" but rather, "Are we courageous enough to use their voices as a gesture of equity and social justice in education?" The Boston and Miami projects set the empirical and conceptual foundations for the third project—The
PRAXIS Project. What is particularly notable about The PRAXIS Project is
that it was not only launched on the West Coast, but also in my hometown,

where I returned as a professor at California State University, San Bernardino in 2009.

The Inland Empire: The PRAXIS Project

The PRAXIS Project—Participatory Research Advocating for Excellence in Schools—was launched as a school-based, university-affiliated research collaborative aimed at recognizing and responding to the education crisis facing the Inland Empire. The Inland Empire, including San Bernardino and Riverside counties, is home to nearly 5 million people. Nearly 80% of the school-age population is either African American or Latino, over 30% of the students are English Language Learners, and the community is faced with a 50%-plus dropout rate. Educational attainment figures are dismal, especially among communities of color. Less than 10% of adults between 25 and 29 years of age have a bachelor's degree, and year after year, less than 20% of high school graduates are eligible for the CSU (California State University) or UC (University of California) systems. Beyond education, the region faces a crime index that is twice the national average, a 15%-plus unemployment rate, and in 2010 *Time* magazine identified the Inland Empire as "Ground Zero" in the national housing crisis.

PRAXIS was launched at Martinez High School in a small, urban California district located in a city of about 60,000 people. Martinez High serves over 3,300 students with a majority-minority student population. Latinas/os comprise over 80% of the student population, with African Americans, Asian Americans, and Whites making up the other 20%. Two-thirds of the student body qualifies for free-reduced lunch, and nearly one-third of the students are English Language Learners. Given the demographic transformation of the region, Latino immigrant student enrollment has maintained a slow but steady increase over the last decade. The vast majority of the teaching corps is White and middle class, although there has been a steady increase in Latina/o teachers over the last several years.

Despite the school's diversity, one can find at least two worlds within the school. For instance, there are the students who are in the Honors and Advanced Placement courses (AP), and those who are in the general nonselective track. Despite 20-plus years of research showing the detrimental effects of tracking or "leveling," segregation by student achievement is alive and well. However, there are efforts to address this disparity.

For example, The AVID Program—Advancement Via Individual Determination—is one of the school's anchor programs aimed at serving low-middle achievers interested in college. There are currently 500 students (about 15% of the entire student population) in the program. Program leaders would like to see the program expanded, but there are several barriers, including resources and staff buy-in. Nonetheless, the AVID program at Martinez High School was identified as one of the most successful programs in the region and state, which can be attributed to the commitment of the program's coordinator, program teachers, and school leadership.

Once a California Distinguished School in 1986, Martinez High continues to face many academic, budgetary, and cultural challenges. While there are always a small group of successful students that matriculate into four-year colleges from Martinez High, a large number of graduating seniors either enter the workforce; attend private, for-profit, two-year schools; have uncertain community-college plans; or do not have much of a plan at all. For decades, it has been the case that only half of all entering freshmen actually graduate four years later. Each year, about 1,100 students enter as freshmen, but only 500 students walk across the stage four years later. While the dropout crisis is on the radar for a select number of school administrators and counselors, there has been relatively little intervention into this crisis. The larger community and many teachers seem to be unaware of the school's dismal graduation rate. It is as if the 500-plus students that disappear over the four-year span between the freshman and senior years constitute something that is expected or simply overlooked. When one administrator was asked about what happens to those 500-plus students, the response was one of uncertainty. While we are fully aware that schools cannot address this challenge alone, a question driving The PRAXIS Project is: What *can* schools do? What is possible, given the many challenges facing the region?

Convinced that schools indeed make a difference, particularly for students and communities that fit the profile of the Inland Empire region, The PRAXIS Project began. After spending the previous eleven years on the East Coast and delving deeply into the issues related to urban education, equity, and action research, I returned to my community and my alma mater high school. This distinction between my East Coast experiences and my journey home is particularly important to note, in comparison to my previous projects in Boston and Miami. For instance, nearly 20 years after my high-school graduation, the challenges and issues that my friends and I had back then still remain. It is because of this intergenerational stagnation, and due to the fact that many of our university-based researchers continue to live in the area or have family members attending Martinez High School, that the stakes were and continue to be high, and served as a motivational force to inspire our work to combat the dropout crisis at Martinez.

This explains, in part, why The PRAXIS Project is inherently critical. The fact that we have been explicitly trying to respond to the pervasive dropout crisis has certainly been a challenge. However, our goal is and has been to develop constructive initiatives through research-based solutions to the challenges facing schools and communities in the region, starting with Martinez High. We believe that in order to address the numerous challenges facing students, schools, and communities, we need to be transparent and public about the inner workings of school life.

As researchers, we could have easily administered a wide-reaching survey in an attempt to understand what is going on in the school, and in many schools, for that matter. However, we decided to roll up our sleeves and prioritize the voices, experiences, and perspectives of those that our system serves—the students. What we found was nearly identical to the findings in Boston and Miami. All together, these three projects across three cities are meant to trigger a national and community-wide dialogue and opportunity to develop efforts to build excellence and equity in schools and communities that have struggled historically.

(Re)entering Martinez High

In December 2009, the principal of Martinez High School contacted me, as he was interested in collaborative efforts to help improve the overall quality of education for all students at Martinez. As an alumnus of Martinez High, an educator, and an urban-education researcher, I proposed that we focus on efforts that respond to the dropout and/or graduation-rate crisis through school-level, research-based initiatives.

Launching on the heels of the Boston- and Miami-based projects, the common thread across all three projects included the power given to the voices and experiences of low-income students, particularly African American and Latina/o youth. I rooted this work in educational research that supported the notion that historically marginalized youth are often the most neglected and voiceless when it comes to educational reform. Our project finds this reality to be counterintuitive and counterproductive to educational equity and excellence, especially because the people most directly affected by the theories, policies, and practices in education—the students—have been the least consulted group in determining, examining, and evaluating educational policy and the effectiveness of reform efforts. Thus, PRAXIS was launched at Martinez with the intention that we contribute to this research base, but more importantly, to help inform school, district, and state-policy formation, pedagogical decision-making, and school and classroom practice.

The PRAXIS Team

As the principal investigator of PRAXIS, I supervised six researchers and student assistants currently in college (CSU, San Bernardino, UC-Riverside, Riverside Community College, and San Bernardino Valley College) or graduate school across the Inland Empire. The members of the team include four Martinez alumni from the 1980s, 1990s, and 2000s, and one as recent as 2011. The research team also includes the teacher-on-record and the entire group of student researchers (described later in this chapter). Our partner teacher was and continues to be a student-centered and pedagogically gifted teacher who is sought out by students on a daily basis. He pushes critical thinking, and was integral in making our work relevant and accessible to students and the school community.

In agreement with school administration and our partner teacher at Martinez High, we worked with two Multicultural Issues classes twice per week starting in January 2010. During year 1, we worked with 76 students in total (year 1). These particular content areas were selected because of the curricular flexibility associated with these social-science electives for 11th- and 12th-grade students. After engaging students in several pedagogical activities, a contest was held, and Year 1 students creatively named themselves, *Students Encouraging Change Through Our Research* (*SECTOR 45*, periods 4 and 5). During the 2010–2011 school year (year 2), we partnered with a new group of students (34), and concentrated efforts with just one class, due to scheduling and accessibility. During year 2, the group assumed the name, The PRAXIS Project.

Theoretical perspectives driving PRAXIS.

The PRAXIS Project was driven by several theoretical perspectives. Like PROS in Boston and POWER in Miami, a major influence is drawn from the work of Paulo Freire. Freire believed that education was either driven by a "banking" method that encouraged fact memorization, or by a more liberatory pedagogy, focused on critical thinking, reflection, and critical action that provides all participants with opportunities to read the word and the world. As Shor (1993) explained, the difference between the banking method and the liberatory approach is the difference between having "something done to them [students]," not something that is done *with* students (p. 26).

According to Freire, an exciting, engaging, and relevant educational experience encourages students and teachers to use problem-posing methods that encourage students to capitalize on knowledge from their own lives by connecting real-life issues with academic content. In these classrooms, students are encouraged to ask critical questions, create and own knowledge, and work to realize democratic processes in classrooms and in society. The goal is to create spaces where students learn by "recreat[ing] the way we see ourselves, our education and our society" (Shor, 1993, p. 26).

PRAXIS was also informed by other critical frameworks, such as Critical Race Praxis. For instance, we allowed students to provide counternarratives, using their voices and experiences as sources of legitimate knowledge—a source that has been historically silenced. To do this, we followed several guiding principles, including:

(1) An examination of race, class, gender, language, and other critical social categories that significantly impact the educational environment,
(2) The need to question long-standing explanations of the achievement and underachievement of historically marginalized groups,
(3) A commitment to examining and incorporating the knowledge of students and teachers, and
(4) A commitment to transformation and social justice (Solorzano & Yosso, 2001).

For example, in our engagement of students, we were conscious of the representative voices in the room by race, generational status, language, gender, class, and sexual orientation. We were aware that voices of immigrants and English Learners can easily be drowned out by their U.S. born Latina/o counterparts. Similarly, we were also conscious of economic differences and gender dynamics. We also challenge dominant ideology, particularly through the curriculum, by introducing more culturally, contextually, and historically relevant stories to students at Martinez High. Our curriculum not only disrupted traditional constructions of history and knowledge, but included pedagogical activities that were committed to deliberate positive change. We discussed the transformative role of teachers and the significance of student-teacher relationships, and gave credence to the lived experiences of students and teachers who were typically excluded from such dialogues.

Research Design and Theory of Action

The PRAXIS Project was driven by a two-tiered methodological process. The first level involved an understanding of student (dis)engagement and achievement from the perspectives, voices, and experiences of students. At this level, the methodology was relatively traditional within the qualitative research paradigm (Level 1). That is, we focused on observations in classrooms and interviews with students, and we used publicly available data to understand the student experience. We blended phenomenological data-collection approaches with grounded theory analysis (Creswell, 2012).

The second level of research revolved around Participatory Action Research (PAR) methodologies and pedagogies (Level 2). At this level of research, we taught students how to conduct research by identifying a topic, framing a question, designing a study, analyzing the data, and disseminating the findings. Our PAR methodology was informed by the work of many scholars, including Youth Participatory Action Research (Cammarota & Fine, 2008); Critical Pedagogy in urban communities (Duncan-Andrade & Morrell, 2008); youth-centered PAR (Rodriguez & Brown, 2009); and PAR Entremundos (Ayala et al., in progress; Torre & Ayala, 2009).

Level 1 research approach.

Upon entry into the school, we informed students of the primary objectives of the project:

(1) To engage high-school students in research opportunities that give them a voice to address student-engagement issues in school, and

(2) To allow researchers to understand how participation in these processes will impact student engagement and achievement in large city high schools such as those located in the Inland Empire.

Parent consent and student assent were acquired, and all university IRB approvals were acquired as well. The objective of the project was to expand understanding of the role of meaningful student engagement to mediate against student failure and produce critical, high-performing, college-bound students. Through qualitative methods, our research aimed to identify specific practices that engage and alienate students from school, and to offer insights into how high school students meaningfully engage with school (Maxwell, 1996). Thus, PRAXIS was driven by the following three overarching research questions:

(1) What are the root causes of student (dis)engagement across two classrooms of high school students in a large, public high school in the Inland Empire?

(2) In what ways can these students best be engaged to mediate dropout and promote student success (i.e., boost graduation and college-going rates)?

(3) To what degree can the lessons learned from this project be utilized to guide our understanding and prevention of student dropout at the school, district, and national levels?

Using a primarily qualitative research approach, the research from The PRAXIS Project sought to establish a model that could be used to reduce dropout among the students who have been historically left behind. By utilizing the voices and experiences of students, we hypothesized that the research process itself will help promote the process of school engagement for students.

Level 2: Participatory Action Research (PAR) approach.

Participatory Action Research (PAR) is a methodological and pedagogical approach rooted in engaging historically marginalized communities in research, knowledge-creation, and advocacy to positively impact school and community change. Its roots exist in both Europe and Latin America. Our approach is rooted in the "Southern" tradition that recognizes the indigenous, cultural, linguistic, and historical contributions of scholars, thinkers, and researchers from Latin America, the Caribbean, and the American South who have helped define and shape the origins of Participatory Action Research (PAR) as a research methodology (see Ayala et al., in progress).

PAR with youth in the classroom aims to engage students in research and advocacy efforts to positively transform school-level practices and policies. Whereas traditional research (Level 1) typically centers the researcher through the research process, the PAR process values, seeks, and capitalizes on the students as researchers (Rodriguez & Brown, 2009). Students develop research topics, research methodologies, collect data, analyze data, and present their findings to relevant stakeholders. Much as graduate students are trained in PhD and EdD programs, we taught students various types of data-collection techniques, and the students decided which approaches made most sense to them. With regard to the research topic(s), we used dialogical pedagogies by posing critical questions to students, such as, Can you identify one empowering or disempowering experience in school? Or, Why do some students graduate and why do some drop out? These questions generate rich discussions, and become the basis for the topics of research explored by the students. Once a short list of research topics is identified, students assemble themselves in groups based on topic of interest and begin to develop a research plan and timeline.

Through the process, the students were required to identify a facilitator, someone who keeps track of information and paperwork, and others who are committed to data collection, analysis, and building the presentation using multimedia sources (i.e., PowerPoint, video and still cameras, and tape recorders). As a way to keep students engaged, the research team remained committed to using history, student voice, the research process, and discussions about consciousness to boost student engagement and achievement throughout the process.

To do this work, The PRAXIS Project was also driven by four core principles:

(1) Using context-relevant and inquiry-driven curriculum,
(2) Participatory engagement,
(3) Liberatory pedagogy, and
(4) A commitment to individual, school, and community transformation.

One way to practice context-relevant and inquiry-driven curriculum to engage students was to first recognize the dropout crisis in the Inland Empire. Then, through problem-posing dialogues, we triggered participatory engagement with students, which was our second guiding principle. Because schools are under tremendous pressure to produce test scores, teachers and the culture within schools generally struggle to provide rich opportunities to dialogue about matters other than tests, especially in low-level and remedial courses. Of course, there are always exceptions, and we have witnessed dialogue-rich classrooms that pushed beyond the heavy test-driven environment to which many succumbed.

We also prioritized dialoguing as a methodological and pedagogical tool, and usually had little trouble getting students to share their ideas and perspectives. We dialogued as a means of ensuring that our effort is participatory every step of the way. Through our participatory work, we aimed to engage *with* students, not over them or on their behalf. We firmly believe that all classrooms need to be participatory.

Thirdly, our work was driven by liberatory pedagogy through the use of problem-posing questions, recognizing students as intellectuals and builders of knowledge, and providing avenues for students to reposition themselves as owners of their education and the schooling process. Finally, all of our efforts were transformative, as we aimed to meet social-justice outcomes by reframing the role of students in the educational process, encouraging students to define the parameters and goals of schooling. We also aimed to achieve outcomes that were more equitable, community-oriented, and always driven toward excellence. Through all of this, the ultimate goal was to boost student engagement and achievement, reduce dropout, and promote graduation and college-going rates in large numbers. Figure 3.1 is a visual representation of our methodological approach and the driving principles behind our theory of action guiding PRAXIS.

Figure 3.1. Praxis Research Design and Theory of Action

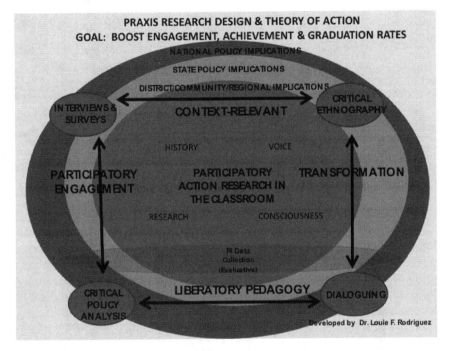

Limitations of The PRAXIS Project

Like any research initiative, there are several limitations to our study. Due to time constraints, we were not able to measure progress over time, and there was limited access to certain types of data, such as real college-going rates of exiting high school seniors. We also focused our analysis on school life, and we recognize that parents and families are a vital component of students' lives. While we find their perspectives important, we are also cognizant of the real challenges facing many working families in the Inland Empire—a struggling economy, a high unemployment rate, and transient living situations. Families struggle with health care, childcare, and transportation. While all of these factors are critical, we wanted to argue that despite these conditions, schools matter. The question is: What can schools do and what are schools doing to respond to this larger crisis? Finally, we did not engage in an in-depth study of teachers and their perspectives and experiences. We value teachers, and recognize the tremendous pressure they are under to help schools meet Adequate Yearly Progress (AYP) targets, Academic Performance Index (API) improvements, and the like; and we know that many teachers persist and excel, even in high-poverty, high-minority high schools. However, our primary purpose was to listen to students, our school system's main priority. The strength of PRAXIS is its concentrated investment in and analysis of the challenges and promises in a school and community context similar to many others that represent thousands of students across the United States, particularly those that serve low-income communities of color.

Pedagogical Approaches

Using Participatory Action Research (PAR), PRAXIS strategically selected pedagogical and curricular experiences designed for and with the students. We arranged our approach around four key experiences we find to be crucial to the development of critical, reflective, and action-oriented student-researchers. These elements were refined over the last 10 years, and began with that initial project in Boston (PROS). The four elements (see Figure 3.2) were:

(1) Educational journeys,
(2) The history of educational inequality,
(3) Powerful ideas in education, and
(4) The group research project.

Such efforts positioned student-researchers in a way that allowed them to develop a critical consciousness about salient issues relevant to the condition of education in the United States and their communities, while also developing a skill set involving research, public speaking, group work, and envisioning their future. In many respects, these efforts allowed students to acquire the "basic skills" that will be transferable to college, the workforce, and life.

Figure 3.2. PRAXIS Approach

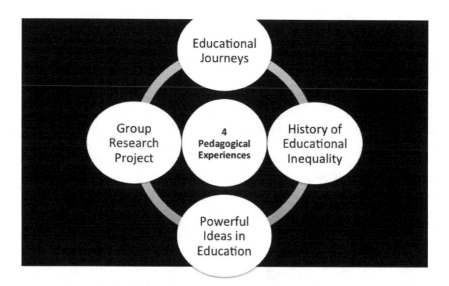

The PRAXIS Approach

Educational Journeys

Group Research Project

4 Pedagogical Experiences

History of Educational Inequality

Powerful Ideas in Education

Educational Journeys

The Educational Journeys exercise is a pedagogical and curricular tool that reflects the values, beliefs, and principles that drive The PRAXIS Project. The idea was inspired by a similar PAR project led by colleague, Dr. Tara Brown, at the University of Maryland, College Park. Her project was titled ARISE, and engaged youth in research in the Washington, D.C. area. These journeys brought to life Freire's statement that, "the starting point for a political-pedagogical project must be precisely at the level of the people's aspirations and dreams, their understanding of reality and their forms of action and struggle" (Freire, 1998, p. 214). In recognition of this, the Educational Journeys aimed to provide students with the opportunity to reflect on and represent key moments in their own educational journeys that were most significant. Students are encouraged to identify both positive and negative experiences and capture those experiences on a large piece of chart paper. Some students elected to write poems, constructed PowerPoint presentations, or created musical lyrics. To initiate the process, I presented a very personal overview of my own educational journey, which seemed to inspire others to open up, build community, and collectively position themselves in a vulnerable role, presenting to complete strangers about personal educational experiences. Oftentimes, the educational scars that students had endured within the school system were shared, as well as moments of triumph and success. It was not uncommon to witness tears of pain and joy shared during the student presentations.

The purpose of the Educational Journeys was to begin the process of getting students to reflect upon and analyze their own educational experiences, and it served as an opportunity to find commonalities across our lives and experiences. We began to see patterns of empowerment and disempowerment that are caused, perpetuated, or challenged by students' experiences in school. We used these experiences to trigger dialogue about root causes to problems, and then posed a series of questions based on their experiences.

History of Educational Inequality

By and large, the history of people of color and their role as builders of knowledge and their contributions to the development of our democracy are largely excluded from the curriculum and pedagogical practices in the K–12 school system. Thus, we aimed to provide opportunities for students to explore relevant moments, court cases, and key figures and movements that have helped shape the path to educational equality and the struggle for equity in U.S. schools and society. Thus, we cover history that privileged the history and perspectives of African Americans, Latinas/os, Native Americans, Asian Americans, and women. Below is a list of topics covered:

(1) *Plessy v. Ferguson* (1896).
(2) Great Debate between Booker T. Washington and W. E. B. Du Bois (1895–1925).
(3) The history of Native American education and the Boarding School Movement.
(4) Women in education and suffrage.
(5) *Lopez v. Seccombe* (1944).
(6) *Mendez v. Westminster* (1946).
(7) *Brown v. Board of Education* (1954).
(8) Chicano Walkouts of 1968.
(9) Boston busing and desegregation court order in the 1970's
(10) *Plyer v. Doe* (1982)

In addition to reading and discussing the cases, students were assembled into groups and "acted out" their specific case. They were given creative license to communicate the core elements of the case in a three-minute skit, mini-play, or a method of choice. This effort aimed at acquiring a deeper understanding of the cases, and students were able to use their creative energy to communicate the case to the entire class.

Powerful Ideas in Education

Another pedagogical approach to our work was to engage students in perspectives about education, schools, and society that are likely to have been overlooked or excluded from traditional curriculum. In many ways, we shared what many critical scholars share with university students, particularly those in certain teacher education and graduate programs across the country. The primary purpose was to expose students to the language and ideas that helped guide the purpose of The PRAXIS Project. These key texts and authors include:

(1) "From Racial Stereotyping and Deficit Discourse Toward a Critical Race Theory in Teacher Education" by Daniel Solorzano & Tara Yosso.
(2) *Pedagogy of the Oppressed* by Paulo Freire.
(3) *Teaching to Transgress* by bell hooks.
(4) *Other People's Children* by Lisa Delpit.
(5) "Social Class and the Hidden Curriculum of Work" by Jean Anyon.
(6) *Subtractive Schooling* by Angela Valenzuela.

By engaging with these key texts, students were encouraged to discuss, analyze, and connect these ideas with their own schooling experiences.

These theoretical foundations served as the basis by which they began to connect their Educational Journeys, theory and research, and their current schooling experiences to shape a research topic for the group project.

Group Research Project

The group research project was the essence of The PRAXIS Project at Martinez High, and like the Boston and Miami project, served to galvanize the students. Before organizing themselves into groups, students identified critical issues at Martinez High. Then, based on topic, students selected a group, and committed to engaging in a long-term (2–3 months) research effort around that topic. Students shaped the research questions, identified participants, selected data-collection methods and data-analysis techniques, and identified implications of their work. All students were required to present their findings to the class, and were given the option to present their research to the school, school board, and community stakeholders.

Key Findings

The findings section will be divided into two levels. The first set of findings will be derived from our survey data taken from a core group of juniors and seniors we worked with over a two-year period. The second set of findings involves research conducted directly by students.

Level 1 Findings

Martinez students have something to say. Before entering Martinez High, we knew that students' voices mattered. However, in our "pilgrimage of the obvious" (as stated by Freire), we knew that we would need data to substantiate what we already knew. Thus, we wanted to know the extent to which students felt that their school sought out their voices to inform school policy and practice.

Among the students surveyed, over 66% stated that they had ideas to improve Martinez, and over 75% said that as future graduates of Martinez High, they agreed or strongly agreed that they would be willing to improve Martinez High. Students are an important resource that teachers, the school, and the district should capitalize on. Who is better suited to provide feedback and ideas about school than current students? Also, who is more committed than alumni who have an affinity for and commitment to the school and larger community?

While our data suggest that nearly three-fourths of the students surveyed have ideas and are willing to improve the schools, less than one-third (<33%) actually stated that they have opportunities to meaningfully participate in school. We obviously need to capitalize on the energy and insight of our students in order to learn from their experiences and engage them in the process.

Challenges and strengths of the school climate at Martinez High. When it comes to the overall school climate at Martinez High, we asked questions about school pride, academic preparation, and the overall "feelings" toward school. The results were mixed. For instance, when students were asked if they would be willing to send their own children to Martinez High, nearly 75% either disagreed or strongly disagreed. Stakeholders should be aware of how their students' experiences in school impact the school's overall image.

We also asked students, if they could do it all over again, would they attend Martinez High. About 40% of the students strongly disagreed or disagreed, and about 60% agreed or strongly agreed. Obviously, more students were slightly more favorable toward the school than not.

Another theme within the literature is the relationship between school size and a student's sense of personalization, or what I later framed as recognition in school (Rodriguez, 2012). Typically, in large high schools across the United States, particularly those in large, urban centers, a school's enrollment, particularly large numbers of students, is typically correlated with higher dropout rates, lower attendance rates, lower student achievement, lower rates of student involvement with school, and higher rates of school violence. In large, urban high schools, which are known to serve most low-income students of color and specifically Latinas/os, English Learners, and immigrant students, students also report high rates of feeling invisible or feeling that people, especially school adults, do not know them well. At Martinez High, the findings were generally in agreement with this literature.

When students were asked if adults knew them well, about 56% agreed or strongly agreed, whereas 44% (or nearly half) strongly disagreed or disagreed. This is critically important to note for several reasons. For the students who feel known, educators should take notice and learn from these students' experiences. Conversely, for the 44% who do not feel known, we need to consider how feeling known is associated with knowing about opportunities in the school and community, accessing college information, knowing what resources are available, and connecting with people who can make things happen—what the literature calls *social capital*. It is also critical to note important research that shows why students drop out or get pushed out of school. Research from the Gates Foundation surveyed dropouts and asked why they left school. Following boredom, feeling anonymous and feeling as though no one cared were among the strongest reasons why students left school (Bridgeland, Dilulio, & Morison, 2006). We cannot overlook the fact that nearly 50% of the students at Martinez High do not finish on time, and students' feelings of being known and cared for should be recognized by teachers, administrators, district officials, and the community. Building connections and relationships are vital but rarely explored in teacher-education programs, professional development sessions with in-service educators, or district policy. Why? It is difficult to mandate caring or the need to know students. While many educators are well poised and skilled to reach low-income students of color, how do we ensure that this is a priority in every classroom and school serving this population, especially when the research shows that it is vital to student engagement and achievement? Perhaps school staff and school-board members should brainstorm ways to prioritize student-teacher relationships in schools.

The finding from "feeling known" is also supported by a question about whether students "feel like a number" in school. The findings were nearly identical, in which 54% of the students surveyed agreed or strongly agreed that they felt like a number, whereas roughly 46% strongly disagreed or disagreed. Again, feeling like a valued member of the school, especially in large high schools such as Martinez High, should be understood and critically examined to determine whether the presence or absence of recognition is impacting student engagement and achievement in school. Some research actually shows that it is necessary for teachers to develop relationships with their students before delving into the academic content (Rodriguez, 2003). This challenges traditional approaches to engaging students, where many educators believe that teachers develop relationships and connections with students solely through the curriculum.

We also asked students if they were proud of being a student at Martinez High. Nearly 66% (two-thirds) of the entire group of students surveyed said they were proud. Pride is a broad term and could be influenced by students' connections to school through sports, clubs, bands, or other activities. Pride could also be influenced by one's level of city pride, which is understandable, given a city's history, size, and culture. So, even if students may struggle academically, they may still harbor a healthy amount of school pride, which is hopeful, and is something educators should capitalize on in serving students.

Martinez High teachers were strongly praised. Another factor to consider is understanding the impact of teachers on students' experiences in school. While the research shows that poverty, parent education, and parent income are strongly correlated with dropping out or succeeding in school, the research shows that teachers are the single most important factor that can eliminate the effects of poverty, especially when students have excellent teachers over a long period of time (year after year). This is especially true for students of color who come from low-income and working-class families (see Conchas & Rodriguez, 2007; Stanton-Salazar, 2001; Valenzuela, 1999). The research shows that students consider their engagement with school attributable to factors such as teachers' expectations of students, whether teachers are approachable, and whether they feel that teachers care. The findings at Martinez High were no different.

For instance, when students were asked if their teachers were approachable, over 75% of the students surveyed rated their teachers good or very good in this area. One-quarter of the students surveyed rated their teachers poor or very poor in approachability. Approachability is another important student-identified factor that shapes student-teacher connections and connections between students and the academic content.

Respect between students and teachers is another common theme that emerges when students are asked about factors that mediate the relationships between them and their teachers. In some of my previous work (Conchas & Rodriguez, 2007), we found that respect was a complex issue, and that students and teachers often had entirely different understandings and applications of respect. Teachers who have strong connections with students practice respect as a second-nature attribute, either due to community connection, cultural awareness, or by making the effort to understand how respect needs to be a deliberate practice (see the work of Bartolome, 2002). At Martinez High, about 82% of students surveyed rated their teachers as good or very good at respecting students.

Students were also asked to rate their teachers on passion, encouragement, and how interesting they were as teachers. Arguably, all three can be mediating factors that determine whether or not students choose to develop a relationship with their teachers. Across all three survey items, 66%, 77%, and 74% of students surveyed rated their teachers as good or very good in these areas. This is a clear indication that overall, students recognize the positive strengths extended by a majority of their teachers at Martinez High.

Teachers, administrators, the school board, and the community should recognize the high praise accorded teachers, and we need to find more ways to celebrate and recognize the contributions teachers are making every single day in the classroom. It is also important to note that while a majority of students rated their teachers favorably, we also need to recognize the power of the minority or the 25% who did not rate teachers favorably. In our experiences in many schools, sometimes a small group of negative educators can dominate the culture of the school, even when they do not represent the perspectives of a majority of the educators. We experienced this firsthand during our first presentation to the faculty and staff at Martinez High. This speaks to the power of the school culture, and encourages us to recognize and facilitate opportunities for the dedicated and effective teachers to have a voice. It is clear from the students' perspectives that they perceive their teachers to be committed, encouraging, approachable, and effective in what they do. Again, this needs to be recognized and celebrated, and we need to learn from these exemplary educators.

Level 2 Findings: Student-Researchers' Findings

The students also engaged in a series of research projects related to their experiences, concerns, and ideas about what works and does not work in school. Below is a matrix outlining topics explored, research questions, methods used, key findings, and implications and/or recommendations for policy and practice.

Highlights of student research. There were several notable findings. Below is a summary of key student findings.

(1) **Budget Issues**—the school should provide a suggestion box so students can voice suggestions and concerns about where to spend money.
(2) **School Environment**—cleanliness was an issue, especially in the bathrooms.
(3) **LATE Policy**—should be eliminated due to students' absence in first period.
(4) **Quality Teaching**—English and History teachers were rated more favorably than Math teachers.
(5) **Dropouts**—school should more directly address the issue; found that motivation and teachers are vital.
(6) **Teacher Effectiveness**—78% of teachers were rated favorably by students; energy, patience, and knowledge of material were seen as very important to teacher quality; teachers need to go "beyond the call of duty."

Table 3.1. Sample of The PRAXIS Project's Student Research for 2009–2010

Topic	Research Questions	Methods	Findings	Implications
Quality of Education	What is the overall quality of education teachers are giving their students?	• Surveys (approx. 116 students)	• Most students rated English teachers above Math and History in listening, interactive activities, and whether or not they can be approached. • Students said they received the most help from History teachers. • Math teachers were ranked lowest in almost every category.	• Students feel English and History are meeting their purpose, but they think Math classes need to provide a more comfortable learning environment in order to succeed.
Teacher Effective-ness	How do teachers instruct, and how does it affect students?	• Surveys (approx. 132 students).	• 78% of students rated their teachers as good. • Top three qualities for a teacher: energy, patience, and knowledge of the material. • Only 40% of students believe their teachers care about them. • Biggest motivation for students was parents. • 54% of students said teachers follow the standards helps keep order. • Students believe AP teachers are more motivating.	• Teachers need to go beyond the "call of duty."

What is A Quality Teacher? Students Speak Out

A recurring theme in our work has revolved around the student-identified theme of quality teachers. While many of the students acknowledged poverty, struggling families, histories of academic struggle, and self-motivation, almost every student we encountered identified the significance of quality teachers in their lives and their role in diminishing the effects of any life challenge. After conducting a series of interviews, below are some representative viewpoints that capture the essence of quality teachers from the perspectives and experiences of students at Martinez High.

By and large, good teachers not only provide students with input in the classroom, but they actually engage in creating pedagogical and/or instructional techniques. Melissa, a senior, stated:

> A quality teacher is someone who listens to their students and is actually concerned with what they have to say. They also teach the class, they just don't pass out worksheets. They also take the time to go through the curriculum and teach it to the best of their ability. I think a quality teacher is Mr. D. because he takes the time to come up with creative things for students to do so the students can learn better.

Felipe, a senior, concurs, and adds that quality teachers ensure that students are understanding the material:

> A quality teacher is someone who knows how to teach and knows what they are doing in the field that they are trained in. They understand students' needs. A good example of that is Mr. B. He actually teaches students. He makes people understand various concepts of the subject areas.

In addition to instructional approaches, another set of characteristics revolved around the notion of caring, as demonstrated by a teacher's willingness to provide access to resources and learning opportunities. Adriana, a senior, states:

> A quality teacher is someone who honestly cares about the students and takes their time to make sure the students understand what they are learning. For example, if it's a math teacher, they make sure they don't move on to the next subject until the student has an understanding and takes the time to do it for all of them [students]. A good example of a quality teacher is Ms. L. The course is pretty rigorous and you have to be quick and analyze. She really goes out of her way to try to help. She gives us reference books and does a really good job at teaching. Mr. S.'s class is more of a discussion class and tries to get everyone interested and involved. Ms. B is a really great teacher. She takes the time to give several examples of whatever she is teaching. She doesn't stop explaining until everyone understands it. Even after that she will stay after school.

Relationships were also vital to the description of quality teachers as defined by students. Relationships help bridge teaching and learning but they also humanize the schooling experiences, especially when the teacher "knows where they [students] are from." Juan, a senior, states:

> A quality teacher is someone who has a relationship with the student, more than just teaching but they actually interact with the student. They are on a good standing basis with them. They know where they are from. They teach what they are supposed to teach and they actually help them. They actually teach the work instead of just giving it to them. Mr. S. is one. He interacts with us. He does more than just teaching. He knows where students are from and what's going on with us.

A final characteristic of a quality teacher was the presence of student voice in the classroom, which was also substantiated by the survey data. Allowing students to share their voices and opinions seemed vital to their engagement in the classroom. Jeff, a senior, states:

> A quality teacher is someone who can relate to the students and someone who is good at expressing their ideas and they let the students have a say when they are learning. Mr. S. is a good quality teacher because we have a voice, he lets us think of new ideas…we talk a lot. Most classes are "just do your work." But [in his class], there is more voice and expressions of opinions.

In sum, students, through their voices, experiences, and perspectives affirmed what most decision makers and other adults believe to be a quality teacher—one who can effectively teach their content areas. However, students also believed that creativity in the classroom, caring teachers, teachers who go out of their way, teachers who give second chances, and teachers who allow students to have a voice in the classroom are also vital characteristics. To a large extent, this is what drove the student research presented to teachers that was described at the beginning of Chapter 1. Our research showed that from the perspectives and experiences of students, this kind of teacher—one who does not appear willing to hear students' voices—was difficult to accept.

Impact of The PRAXIS Project: Shaping educational practice and policy

The need to be "public" about what is happening in public schools through the voices and experiences of Black, Latina/o, and other marginalized youth is vital to improving and shaping 21st-century public education in the United States. Not only are schools like Martinez facing a crisis with dropout and/or graduation rates, so are schools across the State of California and the United States. It has always been our intention to not just collect data and talk about the crisis, but actually use our research and lessons learned to shape school, district, state, and federal policies and practices. Thus, efforts to guide change were and are an intentional and deliberate goal of The PRAXIS Project. There have been at least five significant outcomes of our work so far.

Outcome 1: Eliminating counterproductive school policy. After eight years of implementation, the school's late policy (LATE Policy) had been eliminated as of August 2011, as a direct result of our work. Our research, and the student-researchers' work specifically, analyzed, researched, and critiqued the negative impact of the school's late policy. We found that because of the bureaucracy of the LATE process, many students would miss most of their first class, even if they were one minute late. We also found that many students were tardy because of transportation issues associated with complicated family work schedules. Now, teachers are responsible for noting late students, and students can immediately begin class without missing a significant amount of class time. We suspect that the elimination of LATE Policy will reduce failing grades for period 1 for all students that will likely impact student success and graduation rates. During a meeting with the school principal in late August 2011, he noted that our research helped trigger a needed conversation about the impact of the policy, and the 2011–2012 school year began without the LATE policy in place.

Upon reflection, this policy mirrored very similar zero-tolerances that were present in Boston and Miami. For example, in Boston, one of the high schools instituted a late policy requiring late students to bring an adult from home in order to sign in late. This misguided effort obviously gave very little consideration to the complicated home situations that students often live. Many families in Boston had no car and relied on public transportation. If families did have a car, it was shared by their parents, an older sibling, and extended family members. Nevertheless, it was practically impossible for students to bring a parent from home to sign them in to school. Students got savvy and started to find adults outside the school to sign them in. Their "uncle" signed them in, and the substitute who manned the process at the school entrance made little eye contact with the students or their "uncles." After a few weeks of the new policy, one of the administrators noticed a group of homeless men hanging around the front of the school every morning. It turns out that the "uncle" was from a group of homeless men who made a few bucks each morning signing kids in to school.

During my research, I also came across another scenario demonstrating the impact of these shortsighted efforts to get kids to school on time. I was scheduled to interview Juan, one of my research participants, later one afternoon. I saw him before lunch, and he said, "I have a story for you." So, I met Juan at our usual table in the school library. Juan was a middle-achieving Latino student who was not sure if he was going to college or the military. He was a "good" student and was at school every day. On this particular day, he was late because his mom's work schedule recently changed. She dropped him off late after working overtime on the night shift. Once Juan realized that he needed her to sign him in, it was way too late. He also said, "she was barely awake. There's no way she was going to come back to the school." So Juan proceeded to call his friend who was on the 2nd floor of the school at the time. Juan told him that he was on the outside of a particular door, and Juan's friend asked for a bathroom pass, and opened the door for Juan. Juan said, "how about that Mr., kids are breaking into school."

It must be noted that the logic driving these policies was typically based on good intentions. The proponents would say, "these kids need to be here on time," or "they need to learn to get to school on time. That's the real world." However, the message sent to students was one of neglect. Students felt that adults in the school did not care whether they were there or not. Never mind that these types of policies not only are more likely to be present in low-income schools, but also in schools that primarily serve Black and Brown youth. These practices had damaging consequences on the educational opportunities for students, and for some, pushed them further into the streets and into the pipeline to prison. This will be revisited in Chapter 5, where I discuss the need for sustainability.

Outcome 2: Raising graduation rates. The second significant impact of The PRAXIS Project is recognition of the dropout- and/or graduation-rate crisis facing the school. Because 50% of the students fail to graduate each year, one goal of The PRAXIS Project was to raise awareness of this problem and begin a conversation in and beyond the school. After being in the school for nearly two years, the school reported the highest graduation rate in the school's history as of June 2011 and June 2012. In fact, since the beginning of the project, more than 100 additional students walked across the stage in June 2012 compared to when we first started. Although we cannot take sole credit for this increase in graduation rates, we can say that putting emphasis on dropouts and graduation rates may have raised awareness, and encouraged deliberate action to more vigorously promote on-time graduation. We learned that accountability comes in many forms, and our goal of putting this issue on "watch" may have been just enough to hold the school accountable and serve as a source of support, since our goals are the same—to provide a high-quality education to all students at Martinez High.

Outcome 3: Engaging alumni and the community. The third outcome is our ability to mobilize community members around key issues impacting the school and community. In April 2011, we began to form a network of mostly Martinez High alumni who were committed to creating opportunities, transforming outcomes, and promoting excellence at Martinez High. Most of the interested alumni are Latina/o professionals, who are living in the immediate community and beyond, and are committed to engaging in meaningful work with the school.

Outcome 4: Recognizing and celebrating the work of teachers. We firmly support and believe in the work of teachers at Martinez High and across the region and country. Our research demonstrates that teachers are and continue to be one of the most significant, school-level factors that can make or break students' experiences, outcomes, and opportunities in school and in life. Of course, student effort and motivation, parent involvement, and the larger economic crisis facing districts and communities are influential, yet we are finding that the role of the teacher is absolutely vital. By recognizing and celebrating caring, committed, and engaging teachers at Martinez, we hope we have turned the page onto a new culture in our schools where students, school leadership, administrators, and the community are committed to recognizing excellence.

Outcome 5: Impact on students. Our final outcome rests with The PRAXIS Project's impact on students. For many students, their engagement with the project was the first time they had the opportunity to shape the parameters of their learning experience. For others, it was the first time they spoke in front of a classroom or in a public forum. For others, it was the first time they could say, I "feel like my thoughts and ideas mattered to the community." Many of our students were enlightened by the local history or other well-known historical moments. Many students began to question the daily realities of schools—the curriculum, their teachers, and the general purpose of schooling. Some students became upset. Other students were grateful for the opportunities they are afforded every day, given our progress as a country. Our classroom pedagogy, content used in classes, and contact with students provided opportunities to discuss many themes, topics, and issues that they rarely have had the opportunity to discuss in school. In addition, our direct contact alone provided students with opportunities to interact with college students, graduate students, a university professor, and many members of the community, including the superintendent, the principal, school-board members, and the members of the community at large. We believe our impact has been academic, social, and cultural. Below are some of the voices and perspectives of students who participated in The PRAXIS Project:

(1) "It made me feel like my thoughts and ideas mattered to the community."
(2) "It's always refreshing to see other educators show a genuine interest in the well-being of students."

(3) "Made me feel like my voice counts and I have a say and can make a difference."
(4) "It is important because we are stepping a step forward for change."
(5) "I think this is important so that our voices as students can be heard through our communities and to make change."
(6) "I think it is important because we get to do something new and exciting and we also get to show ourselves what we are capable of in class."

Lessons From Youth Across Three Cities: Vital Insights About School Culture

Across the three projects, not only did we provide an opportunity for students to share their voices, experiences, and perspectives, but the learning processes simultaneously allowed students to build academic skills and raise their consciousness about themselves and their communities. Within the context of the dropout crisis, our research suggests that school matters in powerful ways and requires thoughtful, relevant, and courageous action. Our work also suggests that we need to understand, interrogate, and transform what schools do and how they do it. This is the essence of school culture. Fostering relationships, encouraging a culture of dialogue, creating forums for student voices, engaging students as intellectuals, listening to marginalized students, crafting relevant and exciting curriculum, engaging alumni and community stakeholders, and recognizing and celebrating excellence all encompass critical elements of school life that have been identified as vital to student engagement and success. Of course, poverty, parent engagement, testing, class size, resources, and school policy matter, but so do the ways adults and other decision makers *respond to and act upon these conditions, policies, and practices.* School culture teaches us that the solutions to our challenges are likely to be inside our schools. School culture is that powerful.

Chapter 4 provides a discussion of the various ways that school- and community-based forces significantly shape the student experience. These 10 points are a compilation of lessons learned and insights drawn directly from research and action in Boston, Miami, and Southern California. These factors are framed as a 10-Point Plan that has the potential to shape the way researchers, policy makers, practitioners, and community stakeholders respond to, prevent, and intervene into the crisis so that the dropout rate is significantly reduced and eliminated, student engagement is boosted, and schools focus on producing students who have the wherewithal to decide on their future, understand and transform the conditions of their schools, and contribute to the well-being of their communities and society.

Chapter Four

The Hope in Our Schools and Communities: Toward a 10-Point Plan to Respond to the Dropout Crisis

PROS, POWER, and The PRAXIS Project over the last 10 years have culminated in a 10-Point Plan to Respond to the Dropout Crisis in the United States (Rodriguez, 2011). This 10-Point Plan not only allows local schools and communities to rally around particular policies and practices, but each of the ten points also provides conceptual approaches to policy development and further research. Specifically, each of the 10 points can be used to shape and strengthen school cultures so that they provide opportunities to reduce and resist dropout and promote student engagement and achievement. The 10-Point Plan is comprised of the following:

Point 1: Relationships
Point 2: Student Voice
Point 3: Students as Intellectuals
Point 4: Learning From the Canaries in the Classroom
Point 5: Community-Relevant Curriculum
Point 6: Culture of Dialoguing
Point 7: The Struggle to Recognize
Point 8: School Assets
Point 9: Excellence
Point 10: Making Public Schools "Public"

Using the 10-Point Plan

Each of the 10 points will not only provide a snapshot of the research and policy context that supports it, but will also include a series of practical and policy suggestions that can be considered by interested stakeholders. Each section then concludes with a closing thought informed by a call to action.

It is also not the intention of this plan to create an all-encompassing set of recommendations, nor are these points meant to be blindly implemented by local stakeholders. Rather, stakeholders should take each point and use it as a vehicle for discussion at the local level. It is also important to mention that each point can serve as a stand-alone topic. In fact, the format of each of the 10 points was inspired by the "polimemos" (policy memos) concept started at the University of Texas at San Antonio (see www.aahhe.org) Scholars in the field of higher education used the polimemos format to make research accessible to stakeholders outside of the academy. Finally, it is likely that researchers and stakeholders will be able to use one or a blend of several points to inform local responses. In The PRAXIS Project for instance, stakeholders decided to focus on relationships, student voice, and communities of excellence. It is my hope that local communities can take the polimemos, consider their local context, and act.

Point 1: Relationships

The problem. Relationships and connections with other people are critical to our daily lives—at home, at work, and in our communities. The significance of relationships in schools is no different, especially in middle and high schools, and particularly for students from low-income Black and/or African American, Latina/o, immigrant, and English Learners backgrounds (Rodriguez, 2008; Valenzuela, 1999). Across the country, low-income students of color are more likely to live in poverty, attend underresourced schools, and live in communities where their voices and experiences are unknown or marginalized by institutional policies and practices. This is made readily apparent by the significant dropout rate facing these regions. Reports show that 50% of African American and Latina/o freshmen will not graduate four years later. That is, for every 10 freshmen who enter the ninth grade, only five will graduate four years later. In addition, Black and/or African American, Latina/o, and English Learner students also have disturbingly low rates of college attendance and success. This crisis requires all of us who are concerned to be thoughtful, deliberate, and impatient for results so that more of our nation's most valued resource—our young people—are successful and thriving members of their communities and society.

In addition to the effects of poverty and inequitable opportunities to learn, students also face specific challenges that are reflections of the structure and legacy of unequal schooling in the United States. For instance, as students travel through the educational pipeline, their opportunities to meaningfully engage and interact with important school adults drastically changes. In the early years, students have one teacher for seven hours a day, whereas in middle and high school they have seven teachers in seven hours. Across their educational journeys, students also change significantly— psychologically, socially, physically, and intellectually. They face peer pressure, increased academic expectations (even starting as early as kindergarten with the implementation of high-stakes testing), and are challenged to figure out who they are and how they fit in the world.

For many students and families living in low-income communities, high rates of unemployment, poverty, and transient home lives present considerable challenges for family life. Despite these challenges, we need to ask, How do schools respond to this crisis? What can schools do? What explains success among students that live in these conditions? We know that many of our students and families not only rely on schools for an education and a guaranteed breakfast and lunch each day, but these communities also invest a significant amount of hope in what is possible through formal education.

One significant factor that has proven to shape and promote opportunities and academic success is the presence of meaningful relationships in schools. However, we also know from educational policy; universities that prepare teachers and school leaders; district planning; and school-level, professional-development sessions that too much focus is placed on class size, test-taking, behavior management, and lesson planning, and not enough attention is given to the cultural factors within schools that can motivate, inspire, connect, and engage students. Our work shows that relationships may be the "X" factor that can reduce dropout and promote student engagement. Knowledge of this reality should push policymakers, community stakeholders, educational leaders, and teachers to take notice and act at the policy and practical levels.

The research. In 2006, The Bill & Melinda Gates Foundation surveyed high-school dropouts and found that the second most significant reason why they dropped out was because they felt that no one cared about them (the first reason was boredom in school) (Bridgeland, Dilulio, & Morison, 2006). Thus, meaningful relationships and connections between students and adults in schools allow students to access information, identify mentors, and feel more connected to school (Noddings, 1992; Stanton-Salazar, 2001). Basic forms of "knowing" and "talking" are also vital to developing the basic foundations of student-teacher relationships in school (Rodriguez, 2003). In fact, research also shows that in some cases, teachers must engage students in relationships first, followed by an attempt to engage students with the curriculum (Rodriguez, 2005). That is, for some students, getting them to read, write, and do their homework might require a significant connection with the teacher. And sometimes it is not just the teacher. Sometimes the teacher needs to help the student identify with the curriculum. On the one hand, too many times, adults have deficit-oriented views toward students, which often hinder their ability to connect or relate to students. On the other hand, some school adults do recognize that the strengths and skills (e.g., being bilingual) that students bring to school do indeed impact their engagement with and achievement in school.

Across the three regions of the United States discussed in this book, my research specifically found the following:

(1) In some cases, connections between students and adults must precede the curriculum

(2) Relationships driven by care, trust, and respect are vital.

(3) Adults must recognize that students face adult-like challenges and responsibilities and bring those into the school and/or classroom; recognizing, not ignoring, is vital.

(4) Teachers can relate to students by talking to them and providing high expectations and support.

(5) Giving students a voice in the classroom and/or school is an indicator that adults can relate to students.

(6) Employing creative pedagogies in the classroom is an indicator that adults care for students.

(7) Understanding the students and their community reflects that adults can relate to students.

Practical and policy recommendations. Our research suggests that schools (and the communities that surround them) need to reinvent themselves to become relationship-rich cultures, not just buildings full of people that prepare for and take tests. Students tell us that relationships can indeed transform opportunities for them, boost their engagement and achievement, and along the way help them meet any state or district achievement target. In environments where poverty, inequality, and generations of struggle have persisted, relationships can be the one factor that makes the difference between staying in school and dropping out. Thus, relationships not only matter, but they are also high-stakes. The following is a set of recommendations that can be points of discussion, ideas for policy development, and practical ideas for use in schools and communities.

Possible actions related to the power of student-adult relationships and connections in schools.

(1) School leadership should recognize and emphasize the connection between relationships and learning and/or student engagement. Student-adult relationships, connections, and interactions can be the gateway to academic engagement.

(2) Teachers, school leadership, and school-board members should "shadow" a student for a day to see school through the relational lens of students.

(3) Schools need to recognize that for many students who live in poverty, teachers and other school adults are some of the only college-educated adults they interact with on a daily basis.

(4) Schools should highlight teachers who excel at connecting with and relating to students; we already have examples of excellent teachers in every school, but often no one knows about them.

(5) Schools should prioritize relationships just as much as testing.

(6) Schools should start "Relationship Campaigns" in schools.

(7) Districts should create policies that celebrate schools that prioritize the power of relationships to promote student engagement, achievement, and success.

(8) As a community, we need to understand that the presence or absence of meaningful relationships and connections is an equity and social-justice issue.

Closing thoughts. Students who have been the most marginalized in schools and in our country are also the most likely to drop out, fail in school, and not find a direct pathway to college or a career. As a community, we experience missed opportunities and lost or overlooked talent when we fail to engage our students, particularly those who have struggled historically. While there are many programs and initiatives already underway, thousands of students are not connected and are not recognized. Meaningful relationships and connections between students and adults may be the bridge to engaging more of our students. We need to learn from our most successful students and schools. We will see that meaningful relationships do indeed matter. The question is, Do we have the will to recognize the significance of relationships and act so that we move one more step toward creating more equitable opportunities for all of our youth? Relationships are not just a social or cultural artifact of schools. The presence or absence of healthy student-teacher relationships is an equity issue.

Point 2: Student Voice

The problem. Across the three cities, our research affirmed that everyone likes to be heard. We like to be heard especially when we have something important to say. To be ignored or denied the opportunity to be heard often brings frustration. One might even draw the conclusion that people must not care. That person can either raise their voice and deal with the consequences, or remain quiet and sink into a hole of silence and potential invisibility.

Schools as social institutions serve in this capacity, depending on the culture of the school, the population it serves, and the legacy and tradition of the school and community. Within the dropout crisis facing the United States, where 50% of African American, Latina/o, and English Learners do not graduate on time, the degree to which students have voice in schools and classrooms is vitally important.

Across the three regions, students have demonstrated that having a voice is a liberating experience in the classroom and in larger, school-wide settings. However, feeling silenced can be exponentially impactful, and serves as a significant reflection of the values, beliefs, and priorities of the classroom and school environment. It is no surprise to find that within the dropout crisis facing the country, significant numbers of students feel silenced or invisible largely because there are few, if any, spaces in schools and classrooms to talk about their experiences, share their perspectives, and offer their ideas about ways to improve their school and community. In fact, students are lacking spaces to talk about success and what is actually working well in school. This speaks to individual school culture and the culture of education in general. We have found that providing these spaces not only serves as a mechanism to learn from students and listen to their ideas and recommendations to improve schools, but it also serves as a strategy to actually engage students, particularly those that may be on the verge of dropping out.

The research. Over a decade of research has demonstrated that creating deliberate spaces for learning and achievement is vital for engaging our nation's most marginalized students, particularly low-income African American, Latina/o, and English Learner students (Cammarota & Romero, 2009; Duncan-Andrade & Morrell, 2008; Irizarry, 2011; Rodriguez, 2003). Ten years of research across the United States demonstrates that forums for student voices are sorely missing within the school environment. Students often express concerns about a lack of space, a forum, or a vehicle to share feedback, suggestions, or highlights of their educational experiences (Rodriguez & Brown, 2009). While the creation of this type of space is first and foremost structural in nature, it is also a reflection of the cultural norms or values held at the school or district level. That is, how students' voices and perspectives are received, and the degree to which educators and other stakeholders value the information is a strong reflection of the school's culture. It is clear that creating feelings of silence and invisibility is not healthy for any school, and certainly not conducive to student engagement. This reality should be particularly concerning within the context of the dropout crisis, where silencing and invisibility are core experiences for students before they are pushed out of school (Fine, 1987).

In our research specifically we found the following:

(1) Spaces for student voice can be in classrooms or school-wide spaces.
(2) Schools can use these opportunities to shape school practice and policy.
(3) Students' voices, perspectives, and experiences serve as a barometer check on school culture.
(4) Opportunities to share their experiences and perspectives serve as a strategy to engage struggling students.
(5) When students have spaces to share, they feel connected, valued, respected, and engaged; this can serve as a pathway to academic achievement.

Practical and policy recommendations. Over a decade of student-centered research has demonstrated that our nation's most marginalized students become engaged when spaces are created for learning and achievement. Our research confirms this reality. We have found that students thrive in opportunity-rich classrooms and school environments. We have also found that students who have been historically silenced or marginalized can be the school's richest source of insight and information on how to improve schools and schooling. That is, simply listening to the voices and experiences of students is not only symbolic, but can inform leadership and school staff about policies and practices that work or do not work. But listening to students is a major cultural shift. Schools and districts are typically not accustomed to using students as sources of knowledge and information. Policy makers, school leaders, and teachers need to be comfortable with allowing youth and teachers to explore their own lives and realities as curriculum, share power with youth, and provide opportunities for youth to be public with their learning.

Possible actions related to creating student voice spaces and forums in schools.

(1) Schools should implement student-voice circles or forums with a representative group of students, not just high-achieving and engaged students.
(2) Schools should use student input to guide professional development, school policy, and school practices.
(3) Districts should also conduct district-wide forums to capture students' experiences and perspectives, both within and across schools.
(4) Districts should consider student-representation or advisory committees to school-board members and school-level leadership.

(5) Creating spaces for and with students is an equity-minded practice, because silencing and marginalization is associated with dropping out of school; conversely, providing spaces for voice can promote student engagement and success.

Closing thoughts. The act of providing a space is a strong gesture toward engaging the voices and experiences of students. Actually listening and using this information to shape policy and practice is a major cultural shift and step forward in creating equitable schools for all our students. Because of the context in which we live and the many social, political, and economic challenges facing the field of education and our schools and communities, creating forums and spaces to engage students serves as a direct response to the dropout crisis facing schools. Such efforts are not expensive. All these spaces require is a healthy dose of will, a collaborative spirit with a few dedicated educators, and community support. Until we create spaces for students to share, they will continue to express their frustrations with school through misbehavior, academic failure, and eventually not returning to school. If we are serious about recognizing public schools as vehicles of opportunities for students across the community, irrespective of their language, economic status, race, or immigration status, we need to be willing to listen to and learn from our community's most vital asset—our students.

Point 3: Students as Intellectuals

The problem. The saying that "our children are our future" continues to be a commonly held conviction among people across the country. Yet, our children, and poor youth of color specifically, are struggling. In California, where over 50% of all school-aged children are Black and Latina/o, they are also twice as likely to live in poverty compared to their White counterparts, and they comprise over 80% of all incarcerated youth (Children's Defense Fund, 2010). Children's Defense Fund (2010) also found that over 80% of Black and Latina/o fourth graders in California cannot read or complete math on grade level. But California is not alone. Youth-on-youth violence frequently dominates the print and television media, especially in cities like Chicago, Baltimore, Miami, Los Angeles, Oakland, Houston, and many others. The commonality across all these areas is the fact that there is a concentration of poverty and racial segregation, and in some cities, linguistic segregation. Schools in these communities often face inequitable funding policies, irrelevant curriculum and pedagogy, and misguided practices that overlook or ignore the central challenges facing students and the educators that serve them.

However, we cannot paint the situation with such broad strokes. Some of our youth are thriving. Many policies and practices that create opportunity have proven to transform the effects of poverty, historical inequality, and in some cases, immigration status. To counter the effects of the so-called "dropout factories" and defy the disproportionate effects of school suspensions and expulsions on low-income youth of color, we need to expand what works, especially at the school level. While a 50% graduation rate is insufficient, many are indeed graduating, and some students complete the necessary high school requirements that qualify them for direct entrance into (competitive) four-year universities. These students typically benefit from appropriate placement in rigorous, college-level courses (i.e., AP courses); access high-quality programs (i.e., AVID); experience high-quality teachers who have high expectations, furnish adequate support, and treat students with dignity and respect; and usually capitalize on the promise of meaningful and authentic relationships (Rodriguez, 2008; Stanton-Salazar, 2001; Valenzuela, 1999). In cases where students are succeeding and schools are working for at least some of the students, the community and the country need to acknowledge, celebrate, and expand these efforts. This is where hope in U.S. public schools exists.

The research. Students in general are rarely, if ever, asked how school is going for them. Why not create student-driven projects that investigate school policy, curriculum, student engagement, or community issues? While we recognize that many teachers do this every day, it is rarely the culture of the school to use the school and community as the curriculum. In fact, the role of students in the process of educational change has been the topic of inquiry over the last decade, particularly using Participatory Action Research (Cammarota & Fine, 2008; Cammarota & Romero, 2009). In this work, students become active subjects within the research process, and are encouraged to raise their consciousness about themselves and the world in which they live (Rodriguez & Brown, 2009). Students also learn how to identify and frame issues and problems in their schools and communities, create research questions and research design, learn how to analyze data, and produce presentations to be shared with the community. Students learn how to read the word (academic skills), and they learn how to read the world (raise their consciousness) (Freire, 1973a, 1973b; Rodriguez & Brown, 2009).

We have conducted research and written about the impact this process has on students as they transform their roles into public intellectuals. In my work across three regions in the United States (Rodriguez, 2003, 2010; Rodriguez & Brown, 2009; Rodriguez & Wasserberg, 2010), students have identified low expectations, the role of the teacher, and deep concerns about the dropout crisis as key issues facing their schools and communities. In each case, their final presentation to the community, including teachers, educational leaders, parents, students, and community stakeholders, proved to be a defining moment for the students and their various audiences. Across these projects we found that:

(1) Students place high value on opportunities to critically engage in meaningful research projects; the topic should be student-driven, localized, and relevant.

(2) Students enjoy the position of teacher; they are accustomed to being spoken to or at; when given the space, they demonstrate insight, introspection, and honesty.

(3) Safe and receptive classroom and school environments make these opportunities possible.

(4) For many students, their identity and ownership over the educational process is transformed; they often feel that they control their future after involvement in these projects.

Practical and policy recommendations. Across the three cities mentioned in this book and based on the work of researchers who have been engaged with this work for over a decade, we know what kinds of experiences our students need to be critically engaged with learning, school, and their communities. With the support of educators, community stakeholders, and university partners, local, regional, and state level policy makers need to develop policy that focuses on the *processes* that are necessary to create optimal and equitable learning opportunities for students. Historically the U.S. education system has focused on changing superficial structures and has spent little time focuses on the conditions that are required to allow teachers and students to thrive. Until then, practitioners who are on the ground and doing the work every day will need to continue this necessary work. This point as part of the 10-Point Plan emphasizes that transforming the frame from "student" to "intellectual" is a step in that direction.

Possible actions related to developing youth as intellectuals.

(1) Schools should encourage and support teachers who engage in context-relevant projects that put students in the position of researcher.

(2) Schools should give 20 minutes of time during staff-development meetings to students and teachers engaged in exciting projects to share their progress and findings.

(3) Districts should give school-board meeting time to students and teachers engaged in exciting projects.

(4) Districts should also facilitate opportunities with other community stakeholders and institutions (e.g., mayor's office), inviting them to be the audience for student and teacher presentations, as another gesture to "make public schools public."

Closing thoughts. A "public intellectual" is a label that is usually given to professors, politicians, media figures, and other adults who are often sought out to provide commentary and perspective about global or local matters. Our research demonstrates that creating opportunities for students to be intellectual and public about their experiences and learning not only engages them, but also builds social, academic, and cultural skills to succeed in school and beyond. Excellent examples of this include the student movement within the Ethnic Studies battle in Arizona, and the Watts Youth Collective in Los Angeles. There are countless others, including FUERTE in Connecticut, led by Dr. Jason Irizarry; Project ARISE in Washington, D.C., led by Dr. Tara Brown; the work of Dr. Jennifer Ayala at St. Peter's College in New Jersey; several projects from El Puente in New York City, led by Dr. Melissa Rivera; Dr. Jeff Duncan-Andrade in Oakland; Dr. Julio Cammarota in Arizona; and others in Chicago, Los Angeles, and beyond. Within the context of the dropout crisis, we firmly believe that providing opportunities to be intellectual can be the "hook" that reels students into the classroom and school culture, particularly students who historically have been silenced and disengaged from school. We have come to realize that positioning students as intellectuals is an equity issue, and educators, leaders, and communities should be forthright in creating these opportunities in classrooms across the region and country.

Point 4: Learning From the Canaries in the Classroom

The problem. This point served as a central theme of this book. Within the context of the national dropout crisis, these questions were posed: What is it about the environment that disengages low-income Black and Latina/o youth from school? To build upon Lani Guinier's analogy of the Miner's Canary in the context of U.S. public schools, Who is singing? Who stopped singing? Why? In other words, who are the canaries in our schools and classrooms? What can we learn from them? How can they help us understand the environment so that we can create a healthy environment where all can thrive?

It is widely known that motivated, involved, and high-achieving students are typically the most engaged students in school. Because of previous academic preparation, involvement in special programs (e.g., AVID), and enrollment in highly selective courses, such students essentially assume the identity of a "good" student, and often find themselves on a pathway toward academic success. These students are likely to be involved in school activities such as the student council, sports, or band. These students have also heard about the SAT test, early college admissions, the FAFSA, and why it is important to go on college visits. Because of good behavior and conformity to school rules, procedures, and policies, these students have probably never seen the inside of the vice-principal's office (for discipline problems); have never been subject to in-house suspension; and have never been retained, suspended, or expelled. For these students, school is working for them. Their schools might even recognize these students in some way. Often, these are the students that give educators the motivation to wake up every day. After all, these are the students that are quite easy to engage. They do their homework, listen and participate in class, and are often eager to impress their teachers.

But, what about quiet students, or those silenced by policies, practices, and processes in school? What about the students who are not engaged with school, not involved in activities, and not taking the most selective classes? What about the students who are critical of school, who get in trouble, or who are on the verge of dropping out or transferring to a continuation school. We have found that these students may be the most insightful and reflective sources of knowledge and solutions for school improvement and promoting student engagement. We also acknowledge that across the country students who are marginalized are also most likely to be disengaged, to fail, and to drop out. In fact, they comprise a significant part of that 50% who enter high school but never finish. What would happen if we actually sought out their experiences and perspectives? These are the canaries who have stopped singing in the classroom. Could we reduce dropout and promote engagement in this way? Our research shows that these students not only need to be heard, but may be steps away from entering AP courses, an AVID-type program, or at least being competitive to fulfill all the A-G requirements to meet the standards to enter a UC (University of California) or CSU (California State University) school.

The research. While it is known that disengaged students are likely to attend large schools, live in poverty, struggle academically, and be less likely to have meaningful connections with adults in school, our research uncovers much of what is not known about these students. Our work shows that while the system is committed to providing a structured, safe, and controlled environment for our students, we often fail in understanding or listening to our students and their experiences, especially those that are disengaged from school. Specifically, we have found the following:

(1) For those for whom school is not working, we rarely, if ever, give them a voice.

(2) The most disengaged students often have the most insight about improvements needed in the school.

(3) The most disengaged are typically the most critical of the curriculum and pedagogical approaches used in the classroom; and often for good reason.

(4) The most disengaged students are often the most intellectually capable students, but years of progressive disengagement have trumped their traditional achievements (i.e., grades, test scores), which typically qualify them for competitive programs in high school and beyond; they are sometimes one chance away from engaging with school.

(5) Simply asking the most disengaged students, or even those that are slightly disengaged, to participate can be the "hook" that brings them into the school culture and onto a pathway of academic success.

Practical and policy recommendations.

(1) Schools should deliberately engage marginalized students to learn about their experiences and perspectives in school, and should seek out their suggestions on how to improve school.

(2) Schools should recognize that engaging marginalized students can be the one action that actually engages them with school.

(3) Districts should also seek out marginalized students to understand their experiences, and seek ways to improve schools and the districts.

(4) Districts should recognize that learning from marginalized students is another form of accountability. We need to be courageous enough to seek out, listen to, reflect on, and act upon their experiences in order to improve our schools for all students.

Closing thoughts. If educators, policy makers, and community stakeholders are committed to reducing dropout and promoting student engagement and achievement, especially in large, urban centers where dropout, school failure, and a lack of equitable opportunities to learn are concentrated, then we need to reconsider whose voices and experiences matter. We have found that seeking the voices and experiences of students who might be failing academically, absent from school, or misbehaving might be the source of insight that we need to rethink our policies and practices in schools and in our class-rooms. However, this requires a cultural shift in the way we do things. The naysayers will argue that providing a platform for these students to share is a reward rather than a consequence for their behavior or lack of engagement. We believe that providing that platform may be the much-needed interven-tion that transforms school culture to reduce dropout and promote student engagement and achievement for the country.

Point 5: Community-Relevant Curriculum

The problem. The battle in deciding what to include and exclude from the K–12 curriculum is a long-standing culture war in the United States. The bottom line is that the history of people of color and their role as builders of knowl-edge and their contributions to the development of our democracy are largely excluded from the curriculum and pedagogical practices in the K–12 school system. Specifically, the experiences and perspectives of women and certain subgroups, including African Americans, Latinas/os, Native Americans, and Asian Americans have been largely excluded. While the "culturally relevant curriculum" movement has maintained a strong presence in academic and scholarly circles, it has yet to make transformative policy changes across states and within specific districts (I am not sure that this was the intention, anyway). But the research on culturally relevant curriculum has noted that *what* students learn about actually shapes their engagement and achievement in school. Yet, and in spite of these strides forward, some states have taken a step backward, such that the contributions of specific people have been alto-gether eliminated from the curriculum (as in Texas), or legislators and lead-ership have voted against the inclusion of these perspectives (as in California).

Given that 50% of African American and Latina/o students fail to gradu-ate from high school across the country, a question that continues to linger is, To what degree does the curriculum matter? More specifically, Could a cul-turally and community-relevant curriculum actually serve to engage students in ways they may never have been engaged before? What role do their own experiences and perspectives play in stimulating dialogue and promoting student engagement?

The research. To address these questions, we created a curriculum that had two major dimensions. The first was to allow students to use their own Edu-cational Journeys as curriculum. They told their stories in creative ways us-ing poetry, art, pictures, and media tools. The second explored relevant moments, court cases, and key figures and movements that have helped shape the path to educational equality and equity in U.S. schools and society. Thus, we cover history that privileges the history of African Americans, Latinas/os, Native Americans, Asian Americans, and women. We explored *Plessy v. Ferguson* (1896), The Great Debate between Booker T. Washington and W. E. B. Du Bois, Native American Education, Women in Education, *Lopez v. Seccombe* (1944), *Mendez v. Westminster* (1946), *Brown v. Board of Education* (1954), The Chicano Walkouts of 1968, The Boston busing incident of the 1970s, and *Plyer v. Doe* (1982). Students' experiences and the cases addressed their own struggles and triumphs and the specific efforts to gain equal access to schools and learning opportunities in the United States. While students were generally interested in all of the cases, we found that students had a more focused interest in local cases, including *Mendez v. Westminster* (1946) in Orange County, CA, and *Lopez v. Seccombe* (1944) which took place in San Bernardino, CA. Specifically, we found:

(1) For many students, the Educational Journeys allowed them to share their stories, receive recognition, and feel legitimized, which served as a powerful moment in capitalizing on their knowledge, experiences, and perspectives; this experience largely humanized the learning environment;

(2) Students had no idea that their immediate region played a major role in the struggle for equal schools in U.S. history; students did not know that the *Lopez* and *Mendez* cases actually paved the way for the historic *Brown v. Board of Education* (1954) case.

(3) Many Latina/o students specifically connected with Sylvia Mendez and her sister, especially when the Mendez sisters described how they learned about the legacy of their parents;

(4) Students were particularly struck by the *Lopez* case which restricted the access of Latinas/os to public swimming pools in San Bernardino; this case not only instilled a sense of connection with history, but also ignited a sense of pride in students;

(5) For many students who had been disengaged with our research project, introducing the *Mendez* and *Lopez* cases served as the "hook" that awakened their consciousness; for some, it was the first time they actually raised their voices in our class, or any class, for that matter;

Practical and policy recommendations.

(1) Schools should recognize teachers who do engage in thoughtful, relevant, and outside-the-box approaches to curriculum development. These teachers should help school leadership enhance the curriculum of other teachers, especially when the curriculum speaks to the experiences and histories of our specific students.

(2) Schools should encourage teachers to incorporate historically, culturally, and community-relevant curriculum to engage students, including their own experiences; students often yearn to teach about what they know best—their lives.

(3) Schools can organize panels that include community members that can speak about the history of the school, the community, the region, or any other relevant topics.

(4) Schools can invite school alumni to talk specifically about the school over the decades.

(5) Schools can organize curriculum committees that include teachers, students, and community members to create units on local history; district support and leadership will be essential.

(6) Districts should support schools in collaborating with community partners who can enhance the work of teachers and students in classrooms (e.g., historical societies, notable local leaders and historians, parents and/or grandparents, and universities, etc.).

Closing thoughts. Decades of research and our experiences with The PRAXIS Project demonstrate that *what* students learn can trigger engagement or disengagement in the classroom. This is nothing new. However, our project prioritized a specialized set of learning experiences revolving around the history of educational inequality in the United States, particularly involving the experiences and struggles of communities of color, immigrants, and women. While many students might have heard of *Brown v. Board of Education* (1954) or desegregation, our project provided an in-depth analysis of cases *at the local level.* Students reacted proudly to the contributions of their people in connection with the larger struggle for civil rights in the United States. For some students, engaging with these topics was the first time they raised their voices in class and expressed interest in what they were learning. Within the context of the dropout crisis facing the region and country, we should be mindful of these lessons learned, and be deliberate about what it takes to engage our students, particularly those that historically have been denied access to knowledge and history of their own communities. This could indeed be the hook to reduce dropout, promote engagement, and pave the way toward academic success across the subject areas.

Point 6: Culture of Dialoguing

The problem. It may be surprising to educators and the general public alike that the dropout crisis facing the region and the country is hardly a commonly discussed issue. While there are efforts underway, we have found that confronting the fact that 50% of students in the country will drop out of high school is largely absent from district-led conversations and professional-development sessions at the school level, and is almost never discussed in classrooms. But why? Why would such a glaring problem affecting the quality of schools and the future of our community be overlooked or ignored? We believe it does not have anything to do with malicious intent or outright disinterest. We believe the field of education and our schools specifically lack a culture of respectful, constructive, and forward-thinking dialogues that move us from not only recognizing the problem, but toward coconstructing solutions that are immediately applicable to each school or community.

The culture of not dialoguing can be attributed to the increased standardization in schools (i.e., scripted curriculum) and narrow definitions of knowledge and achievement via the testing culture that has plowed through schools over the last 10 years. These policies and practices have socialized many students and teachers into passivity and authority dependence, rather than developing and promoting critical, creative, and reflective thinkers (Shor, 1993). It is within this policy and cultural context that educators are faced with disengaged students, behavior problems, and many students who altogether drop out physically and/or intellectually. The blame for this progressive disengagement from school is often centered on the student, their culture, or their family's values. Seemingly without recourse, some educators and the general public embrace these misguided assumptions, along with low expectations, misguided educational policy, and a general unwillingness to engage in dialogue with the very people that are impacted by these forces—the students and the community. Thus, the practice of dialoguing has almost become a revolutionary act, but not impossible.

The research. Research demonstrates that classrooms, schools, and other educational spaces that are rooted in a commitment to dialoguing between students, teachers, and communities are highly effective. When students are asked about quality teachers and learning environments, they yearn for the opportunity to be heard, to teach others, and to listen to others (hooks, 1994; Rodriguez & Brown, 2009). Research also shows that students are heard when authentic relationships are a fundamental aspect of the cultural fabric of schools and classrooms, particularly for low-income students of color (see Point 1 of this series).

Yet, the act of dialoguing is a complex undertaking. Many leaders steer away from dialoguing about complex issues such as dropout because of the fear of losing control of the dialogue. In our experiences and across our observations, semistructured and organic dialogues where theories emerge, power is shared, and knowledge is coconstructed are often the most powerful for engaging students. To engage adults in these much-needed dialogues, school leaders need to be bold in raising issues such as expectations and relationships, the experiences of English Learners versus U.S. born Latinas/os, and cultural accountability for student learning. Educators need to realize that talking about race, class, and gender is not racist, classist, or sexist. But if an issue, such as race, is a factor that impedes the ability of educators to serve students, then it needs to be addressed. The first step is to recognize the problem, and create a space to struggle through the issues. It will not and should not be a sanitized dialogue. Tempers will flare, and people will get offended, but a skilled, respectful, and politically committed community should identify support and move forward deliberately and justly. Only through the work of courageous educators will the relevant issues and causes of student engagement and disengagement be addressed.

Struggling through tough dialogues is a gesture toward progress. We experienced firsthand the often sensitive and volatile nature of raising certain issues with schools and communities. During a presentation at a local middle school, some teachers took offense to the research suggesting that teachers do indeed matter when it comes to reducing the dropout crisis. We did not blame teachers, nor did we say that teachers are not doing enough. But we did say that teachers matter. A couple of teachers interpreted our reporting of the research as a critique. With the help of a strong school leader, we respectfully continued onward, and arrived at an understanding that we all share the same goal—to promote excellence and equity for all of our children. While we struggled through the dialogue, such dialogues are necessary. If we continue to ignore the dropout and/or graduation-rate crisis, or the fact that significant percentages of students are behind in credits by the end of their freshman year, or the fact that many students and teachers struggle to relate to one another, we will never move forward as a community or country.

Practical and policy recommendations.

A school culture that promotes dialogues about expectations, relationships, and responsibility will require persistence, support, and courage, especially among teachers and school leadership, along with the support of the community and key policy makers. Many will welcome a much-needed and timely dialogue, while others will slip into the age-old narrative about lack of student motivation or unsupportive parents, or share beliefs about deficit-oriented cultures. It is only through the work of courageous educators that the relevant issues and causes of student engagement and disengagement will be addressed. Below is a set of possible actions related to dialoguing in schools.

Possible actions related to dialoguing in schools.

(1) Schools and districts should dialogue about critical factors attributed to the "opportunity gap," such as student engagement, curriculum relevance, and the dropout and/or graduation-rate crisis.

(2) Schools should expect defensiveness and resistance from the "we already do this" culture within schools; this voice is loud.

(3) Conversely, schools and communities should harness the energy and ideas of forward-thinking educators and community members; these are the most vital allies.

(4) District leadership should support schools in these conversations by ensuring that these dialogues are productive, fair, and that all perspectives are represented.

(5) District policy should support schools that engage the larger community in educational forums as a way to build support within and beyond the school.

Closing thoughts. Dialoguing is one of the foundational principles of our democracy. However, we often find that our schools and communities, particularly those that are consistently struggling, are in dire need of a culture that promotes, encourages, and supports critical dialogues about the most pressing issues facing our students, teachers, and schools and communities. This will take a joint effort of willful leadership, community inclusion, and a respectful process. The solutions to our communities' most pressing problems *already exist* in our schools and communities. These community members are our youth, our parents, our teachers, our grandparents, our elders, our business leaders, our elected officials, and all stakeholders committed to promoting equitable opportunities for all of our children. However, we will never realize the true extent of their power unless we leverage the wisdom, experiences, and creative energy of these community members, and set a thoughtful plan of action to reduce dropout, promote engagement, and create opportunities for student and community excellence.

Point 7: The Struggle to Recognize

The problem. As mentioned in the Preface, my dissertation work at Harvard University focused on school culture across ten structurally different public schools in the northeastern United States (Rodriguez, 2005). In doing my research, I met Ramon, whose experiences were discussed in Chapter 2. An avid reader and writer, and quite vocal about the school's inability to challenge him, he believed that the curriculum was irrelevant and repetitive, and he felt that opportunities to critically discuss the purpose of school were absent. While people knew of Ramon, they really did not know him intellectually. His curiosity and hunger for more engaging opportunities were missing from the school environment. From Ramon's experience I began to ask, Why is Ramon being ignored? What can he teach us about school? From this experience, I created a framework of recognition—the degree to which students (and adults, for that matter) were recognized by school adults across the various domains of schooling, including relationships, curriculum, pedagogy, context, and understanding the purpose of education (Rodriguez, 2012). I discovered that most students fail to have meaningful contact with school adults on a daily basis. Being cognizant of this reality is particularly useful, when students who drop out of school are likely to report that no one cared about them at school (Bridgeland et al., 2006). Learning from the experiences of students over the last 10 years, we believe that students leave school because we fail to recognize their existence on multiple levels.

This Recognition framework encourages teachers, administrators, and community members to question sweeping assumptions that are frequently made about the experiences of students, particularly low-income students of color. For instance, we should not assume that low-income students, African American and Latina/o youth, or English Learners are acknowledged in school. We should not assume that they are greeted or that adults know their names. We should not assume that their voices and experiences are validated within the school context. We should not assume that they leave their communities behind when they enter the classroom. We should not assume that all educators understand that many of our communities rely on public schools to instill hope and opportunity through students. In order to regulate these assumptions, teachers, leaders, and community stakeholders can benefit from a set of counter-assumptions facilitated in part through the *Praxis of Recognition.*

The research. Our research continues to show that many students fail to have meaningful interactions and relationships with their teachers and other important adults. While there are always exceptions, we explored the degree to which students are recognized in schools and classrooms. We found that establishing a Praxis of Recognition (Rodriguez, 2012) within schools is vital, particularly across five key areas:

(1) *Relational Recognition* recognizes that student-adult relationships are vital to student learning and engagement. *We should assume that Black and Latina/o youth, like all youth, benefit from meaningful relationships.* We should be asking, Are students greeted? Are their names known? Is their basic human existence recognized?

(2) *Curricular Recognition* encourages institutions and educators to consider how knowledge and experiences of students may serve as powerful forms of curriculum. *We should assume that low-income students of color are ready to engage in rich, intellectual activities, particularly when the content is directly relevant to their lives.* Are students, their communities, and their histories reflected in the curriculum?

(3) *Contextualizing Recognition* urges us to connect students' dispositions and engagement with school to the large community context. *We should assume that students bring a wealth of experiences, and expect schools to capitalize on these experiences.* Do we understand the role of the community in shaping student engagement?

(4) *Pedagogical Recognition* is exercised through creative and courageous pedagogies that stem from and are shaped by students' experiences in schools, the values they place on particular knowledge and experiences, and how these experiences and life lessons interact within the larger social context. *We should assume that students want to teach about their experiences.* Do we provide opportunities for students to do this?

(5) *Transformative Recognition* urges educators and researchers to ask what the purpose of education is for low-income students of color. *We should assume that students are ready for a new kind of learning experience in U.S. schools, particularly those that have been subjected to years of social, cultural, political, and intellectual alienation.* Do leaders and teachers understand their roles in the lives of students?

Practical and policy recommendations.

Schools can address the following questions:

(1) How do they recognize students, in terms of relationships?

(2) How does the curriculum recognize and reflect the realities of students and the community?

(3) In what ways does the pedagogy allow for knowledge construction among students, and how, if at all, are they allowed to be public intellectuals?

(4) In what ways do our schools recognize and incorporate the contextual realities of the community (i.e., immigration and language politics, history, poverty, economic crisis, housing, etc.)?

(5) How does each school define the purpose of education? How do students and the community define the purpose of education?

(6) Districts should facilitate opportunities for schools to engage in practices and policies that address and effectively respond to these questions.

Closing thoughts. Until revolutionary structural changes are made within our public-school system, schools, educators, and community stakeholders can and should recognize their roles in forging change in schools from the inside out. Also, because dropping out of school is something that happens over time, stakeholders can use the Recognition framework to examine the degree to which their actions and the school's policies and practices are resisting or contributing to student engagement and disengagement, particularly among low-income students, Black and/or African American students, Latina/o students, and English Learners. Deliberately creating schools that acknowledge who the students are, where they come from, and their promise in becoming future leaders should trigger action driven by support, high expectations, and a relentless pursuit of equity and excellence in our schools. We need to recognize that students across the country need committed teachers, thriving schools, and equitable opportunities within and beyond the community to recognize their potential. Practicing Recognition within our schools helps create a culture that pushes us in that direction.

Point 8: School Assets

The problem. When parents and communities are directly involved in the education of their children, students are more likely to engage, achieve, and thrive. This research holds true for all children, especially low-income children of color who historically have struggled in the K–12 system. There are countless examples across the region and country where individual parents and communities serve as powerful advocates for their children, and the outcome is likely to be quite favorable. School leadership and teachers typically find it helpful to know that a child's parents are involved and engaged. However, this is not the norm in our community, and for good reason. A recent report found that the city of San Bernardino has the highest percentage of people living in poverty among all large cities in the State of California, and is second at the national level behind Detroit, Michigan. Families living in poverty not only struggle financially, but they struggle to access the very institutions that theoretically are meant to serve them. Some families struggle to find work, access reliable transportation to get to work, put food on the table, or find a safe place to sleep each night. When living under such circumstances, to be involved or engaged in school is simply off the radar. Some families might even find it a relief that their children have a safe place to go for at least seven hours a day. Thus, it should be no surprise that this region and many communities across the country have low levels of parent involvement. And while there are many programs and initiatives in place, perhaps we need another source of support to advocate for our children—alumni and the community. While the region in general has among the lowest levels of college-degree-holding adults, especially in San Bernardino, there is a small but committed group of successful alumni and community members in general who care about the well-being of children in the local schools, and about the future of the community. These may be among the school's most critical and untapped assets, particularly in larger urban centers.

The research. As we engaged in our work at Martinez High School, we witnessed the development of an incredible movement. Our research began to attract attention from community leaders, parents, and the media. Stakeholders from across the community started to take notice, get involved, and support our work. One significant group has been Martinez High alumni. During our April 2011 community event, we attracted alumni from every decade since the 1940s. At this event, alumni and other community stakeholders such as elected officials, education leaders, parents, students, and school staff began a dialogue about ways that the community can actually get involved in supporting our work and the school generally. We identified three major areas—scholarship support, in-school support, and college and career awareness. We began a conversation about envisioning Martinez High in 2015. We believe that our emerging work in this area is not only beyond the scope of the traditional class reunions or booster clubs for sports that attract alumni, but that engaging alumni and community stakeholders can be the beginning of a significant source of support that triggers systemic change in the school and the community. Specifically, we found the following:

(1) Alumni and community members in general are ready to engage with their alma mater in meaningful ways; they simply need a vehicle to engage.

(2) Alumni and community members may be amongst the most loyal of advocates, given their longevity in and commitment to the community.

(3) Alumni and community members serve as critical allies in research and advocacy work, especially when projects aim to transform school culture and create systemic changes.

(4) Alumni and community members bring a wealth of experiences and resources to schools; however, there needs to be responsive leadership at the school and district levels.

(5) Alumni and community members serve as another level of on-the-ground accountability for schools and districts.

Practical and policy recommendations.

(1) Schools should recognize and engage a powerful, supportive, and resource-rich network—their alumni. Many alumni are passionate about giving back; not just by donating money, but also by sharing their stories and advice for college and career readiness.

(2) Schools should provide "alumni highlights" visibly in the school that celebrate successful alumni, particularly those serving their communities. Students and teachers begin to develop a sense of what is possible in their everyday work in the classroom.

(3) Districts can also organize alumni work groups to support and advocate for the interests of the school. Alumni and other community stakeholders can be critical allies and advocates, especially when school-level leadership, teachers, and other staff are overwhelmed with the day-to-day functioning of schools.

(4) Schools and districts should deploy alumni and community survey teams that observe and support school-related efforts; alumni and community members typically have access to or knowledge about critical resources that can assist the school.

Closing thoughts. Middle-class schools across the country engage parents, community members, and alumni in quite effective ways. While there are examples of low-income schools that also effectively engage parents, it seems timely and necessary to broaden the scope of possible community support to help engage students and transform outcomes and opportunities for those that historically have been left behind. Alumni and community members should be that source of support. Alumni and community members have deep histories and a wealth of knowledge. We need to capitalize on these assets that are often an e-mail or phone call away. Getting alumni and the community to "watch" public schools is not only another form of accountability, but is a potentially powerful source of support and resources for students, parents, and teachers. Recognizing and harnessing the assets of alumni and the community is an equity issue, as it is sure to boost engagement and achievement and help reduce dropout, promote student engagement, and close the achievement gap across the country.

Point 9: Excellence

The problem. Teachers and students do amazing things every day in classrooms and communities. In an era of heightened scrutiny placed on schools due to the standards-based movement and strict policies such as No Child Left Behind, it is too easy to focus on test performance, rather than on genuine learning, teaching, and engagement. That is, the culture of a "Test Prep Pedagogy" (Rodriguez, 2008) has, in many ways, steered us away from recognizing the day-to-day victories in schools and classrooms. Despite the testing culture, there are great things happening even in high-poverty and consistently low-performing schools serving mostly low-income students of color, and immigrant students. The fact that we fail to celebrate and recognize success and excellence more frequently has to do with the culture of education generally and school culture specifically. In the context of the budget cuts, lowered educator morale, and struggling students and families, it seems that the national dialogue around value-added tools to assess teacher performance, reducing class size, or the typical narrative about the "failing" public school only puts our teachers in a corner, reduces students to test scores, and distract us from the real problems facing the school system. Our students, teachers, and parents often bear the brunt of the ills associated with the system, especially in times of crisis. In response to this void, The PRAXIS Project launched an Excellence Campaign™ highlighting community members who earned a higher education, became professionals, and returned to serve their community. Our project's efforts at recognizing excellence among educators specifically was a significant step in the right direction, especially in responding to the dropout crisis facing the region.

The research. The research shows that people appreciate recognition of their efforts. In schools, students appreciate recognition from teachers and administrators, and at home they appreciate recognition from parents and community members. Teachers are no different. We found in our work that excellence is a widely agreed-upon standard but rarely identified or celebrated. Thus, we began to travel around different schools, at the invitation of the schools' leadership, and shared examples of community excellence. We decided to put the concept of community cultural wealth (Yosso, 2005) into action by highlighting people who were serving our communities in powerful ways. We highlighted a Chicana medical doctor, a Mexican dentist, a Latina college counselor, an African American community advocate, and a Chicana middle-school teacher. We created a multimedia presentation including pictures, biographical facts, and moments of struggle. We reiterated the point that excellence in the community is returning and serving the community. We highlighted their educational journeys by noting that they had attended some of the most prestigious universities in the country. The presentation has been shared with teachers, students, and parents, and has been a resounding success. We also made it a point to lead The PRAXIS Project students in a campaign to identify examples of excellence in their school. They identified the most committed, most caring, and most creative teachers in the classroom. In our work, we specifically found that:

(1) Schools need help with creating opportunities to recognize teachers and students; unfortunately, it is a not-so-common practice in our public schools.
(2) Teachers appreciate the recognition, and the gesture serves as a source of motivation and affirmation that their hard work is appreciated by the community.
(3) Students, teachers, and school leaders typically jump at the opportunity to celebrate excellence, especially if they are repeatedly told that they are not meeting the standard.
(4) Celebrating excellence will face resistance; the act of recognizing one or a group of educators will likely go against the cultural fabric of the school; leadership is vital.
(5) Students who feel they are surrounded by excellence will internalize the principle of excellence, and it is likely to shape the school culture.

Practical and policy recommendations.

(1) Schools should enlist "Excellence Committees" that highlight the success and excellence of teachers and other critical adults in schools. These celebrations should be frequent and public. Teachers are some of the most overworked and least recognized of all profes-

sionals. These committees can be student-driven student and teacher collaborations, and also include members of the community, such as parents and other community stakeholders.

(2) Schools should lead the staff and students in efforts to define what success is, and identify examples in the school.

(3) Schools should highlight excellence in the classroom by profiling teachers and students who are excelling. Inexpensive, poster-sized profiles can be created along with school newspaper writers and art teachers.

(4) Students can serve in leadership roles to guide such excellence initiatives; this can serve to engage students and raise their consciousness about school culture.

(5) Districts should recognize excellent teachers and students during every school-board meeting.

(6) Districts should support schools in efforts to publicize teachers and students who are doing great work, especially in the local media.

Closing thoughts. Given the challenges facing education, schools cannot do this work alone. Struggling schools, particularly those in turnaround mode or implementing program improvements, are so preoccupied with meeting the mandates of districts and states that they find very little time to stop and celebrate success and excellence. Our work as a youth-centered research initiative helps to alleviate the school's responsibility for this task by engaging youth in the process, and helping to contribute to a school culture that celebrates excellence. As initiators of the process, we are privileged with the power to shape the process, and therefore frame excellence, as people who are committed to fostering student voice and excellence, particularly among Latina/o and African American students who are disproportionately failing and dropping out of school. Schools, with the help of the community, can easily assume the same role. We believe that celebrating excellence is as much an equity issue as school funding, curriculum, and standard. We are finding that committing to and practicing the recognition and celebration of excellence is a transformative tool that reshapes school culture, and can help reduce dropout and promote student engagement, particularly among students who have been denied opportunities to see themselves as community leaders of excellence.

Point 10: Making Public Schools "Public"

The problem. Public schools across the country are complex institutions, particularly in communities that serve predominantly low-income, immigrant, Black and/or African American, Latina/o, Native American, and English Learner students. In many ways, they are expected to not only get students to achieve, but also to help level the playing field that stems, in part, from decades of social inequality. And while popular opinion may have the general public believe that all public schools are failing, this is far from the case. In fact, there are many highly successful public schools across the country. There are also highly effective public schools that serve low-income children of color (see The Education Trust's website, http://www.edtrust.org, for a list). These schools are typically committed to several core elements that have been known for the last 30 years of research: strong school leadership, high-quality teaching, committed and competent teachers, engaging curriculum, a commitment to relationships in schools, high expectations, and parent and community engagement. Yet, in 2011, we still struggle to ensure that all children are afforded an equitable opportunity to learn. But to achieve equity, we still need to acknowledge that our public schools in the United States are still "public." Those of us concerned with the dropout crisis facing the country need to realize that we need to recognize and respond to the crisis in a public way.

Over the last three years in Southern California, and over the last 10 years in Boston and Miami, there has been one major commonality—what happens in schools largely stays in schools. Aside from the occasional scandal and the yearly publication of standardized test scores, the inner workings of the public schools are largely treated as a private matter. Whether students are being mistreated by a teacher, whether students are not learning about their community, or whether the policies or practices are pushing students out of school, the reality is largely unknown by the general public, especially when the student population is disenfranchised by other social institutions across the community. Similarly, if there are amazing teachers, meaningful student learning and engagement, and student-centered policies and practices in effect, the general public is also, by and large, unaware of this reality. The point is that as a culture, we fail to know or demand to know what is happening in our public schools. Our research aims to address this void.

The research. What happens when initiatives are introduced that actually promote the idea of making public schools "public"? More specifically, what if the voices, experiences, and perspectives that make public schools "public" are delivered by the students themselves? What if alumni and community stakeholders are interested, and help drive the process? Our research has begun to implement a series of efforts that do just that—make the public schools "public."

In my projects in Boston and Miami, and in those of many colleagues in Arizona; Connecticut; Washington, DC; New York; and Oakland, CA, we engaged the voices, experiences, and perspectives of students to publicize what is working and not working in our schools. While small but significant groups of educators and community members have been supportive, we have also faced resistance, especially from people who might have been implicated as ineffective in their approaches to engaging students, particularly students who are more likely to be disengaged or drop out. After almost every presentation, a group of educators would approach us, who are typically teachers of color but not always, and applaud our work. They typically say, "these are the kinds of projects we need," or "we needed to hear this." While supportive, they rarely raise their voice in the larger group. However, the more vocal groups, who are also small but powerful groups, typically critique or question the purpose of engaging in such work. Some get defensive. Some are obviously angry. In other venues, we have presented in front of larger groups of community members, and we have received strong support and encouragement to continue. For many of the community members, the work we share is recognized as valuable, and discloses what many people already know and experienced. Many typically believe in and join our efforts. Lessons learned from our research include the following:

(1) **Students' Voices Matter:** not everyone is ready to listen to the voices of students; some will discredit them; but there are always supporters.
(2) **School Culture Matters:** depending on the culture of the school, making public schools "public" can be warmly received or vehemently resisted; a school's reception or rejection of public matters is a reflection of school culture.
(3) **Silence Matters:** it is easy to misinterpret silence as disinterest, especially after making matters public; sometimes one-on-one outreach helps amass more support.
(4) **Audience Matters:** presenting to audiences comprised of educators and noneducators including alumni and community supporters matters; thriving teachers and school practices need to be recognized and acknowledged by the community, and the community needs to be made aware of the challenges and struggles, so that a community-school response can be developed.
(5) **History Matters:** if schools are not accustomed to publicizing success or what needs improvement, leaders, committed educators, and community members need to push the agenda; there is something

terribly wrong when educators or students are ashamed or uncomfortable with publicizing their success in the classroom.

(6) **Outlets Matter:** in our work, we have used social media, traditional news outlets, and personal outreach to share and engage people in our work; students are particularly proud of their engagement when community members and news outlets recognize and appreciate their work; for many of our students, this recognition communicated to our young people that the community cares about them.

Practical and policy recommendations.

(1) School leadership should get in the habit of routinely recognizing important strides forward and successful teaching and learning efforts in the classroom; we need to flood the public waves with stories of success to not only celebrate our accomplishments, but promote a culture of excellence for students, parents, and the community.

(2) Schools should use their newsletter or school newspaper to highlight some of this work; they can even partner with local journalism or communications departments at local universities to help publicize their work.

(3) Schools facing significant struggles should not feel as though they are alone; community-based partners should help address these struggles by capitalizing on the rich resources already present in the community.

(4) Community members, including alumni, can join efforts with students, teachers, parents, and administrators via work groups in addressing key challenges and recognizing excellence.

(5) Districts and school boards should institute policies that help make public schools "public" by inviting students to give biannual reports and/or speeches on the State of the School from the student perspective; challenges, successes, and suggestions for policy and practice can be shared.

(6) Districts and school boards should publicly share annual college-going rates and graduation and/or dropout rates, and engage communities in goal-setting for short-term and long-term time frames.

Closing thoughts. The lessons learned from the students' voices and experiences across the three cities suggest that there is hope in our schools and communities. Specifically, they demonstrate what needs to be done to improve the culture of our institutions to more adequately respond to the many challenges that exist. While many of the challenges are no fault of the school system alone, there is certainly deliberate action that we can take to equitably create more just learning conditions for all of our children, particularly those who continue to struggle. Appreciating and prioritizing relationships, honoring students' voices, recognizing the existence of our students, learning from the marginalized voices, and deliberately creating excellence are just a few of the 10 points developed from data gleaned across the three cities and discussed in this chapter (see Figure 4.1). If taken seriously at the local level, this 10-Point Plan is likely to stimulate a much needed dialogue and eventually a long overdue transformation of educational policy and practice in low-income schools and communities. To bring these points to life, a significant political process will need to occur. We cannot assume that educators or policy makers know what to do with the 10 po ints, nor should they act in isolation from the community. The 10-Point Plan should be driven by a movement that includes parents, students, educators, policy makers, and community stakeholders. This is the subject of Chapter 5.

Figure 4.1. A 10-Point Plan to Respond to the Dropout Crisis

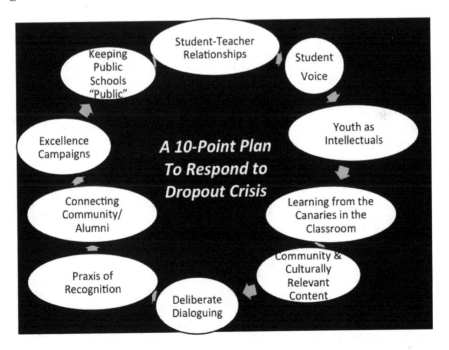

Chapter Five

Keeping the Canaries in the Classroom: Toward a Theory of Action

In order to confront the 50% dropout crisis facing our youth, communities, and society, we need to create conditions in our institutions so that our students not only stay in school but also thrive academically, interpersonally, and intellectually. We heard from students like Ramon in Boston and Tina in Miami who represent two of the 50 million students attending our public schools every day across the United States. We learned that they rise every single day. Sometimes they handle significant household responsibilities before school. They care for younger siblings. They help get parents to work. They care for their grandparents. They take one, two, or three buses to school, jump on the subway, and then walk to school. Before, during, and after school many of our students have to dodge gangs, drugs, or other neighborhood stressors. Sometimes they have to fight the school's policies to get into school, as Juan in Boston shared. Yet, they get to school. They want to succeed. They want to be engaged. They do have a voice. They are seeking relevant and deliberate role models in our schools. They want their classrooms, schools, and communities to validate their experiences. They have something to contribute. They have something to teach. In this book, our students have spoken. But, are we ready to listen? Are we ready to learn? And, are we ready to act?

This book has demonstrated that students are quite forthcoming with what works and what does not work in our public schools. In fact, our willingness to engage and learn from students' voices also ensures that our public schools remain "public." Our research over the last 10 years suggests that teachers are also in dire need of support and recognition of their everyday efforts. After all, they, too, are human, and need the same basic recognition that our students yearn for in the classroom.

In order to push this work forward, schools and communities, including key players such as alumni, will need to play a vital role in publicizing what needs to be improved and highlighting models of excellence that already exist in our schools. Until we establish this culture, especially in our struggling public schools, our students will continue to attend school in isolation from the "public," and the dropout crisis will likely persist.

We also need to be conscious of the powerful impact that school culture plays in shaping experiences and outcomes for our students. Resources, programs, and factors such as class size indeed matter, but so do the ways *we use* these resources, *who gets access* to these programs, and *what actually happens* in small or large classes. That is, we can add money to the pot, create new programs, and reduce class size, but what happens in these structures is also critically important, which is why we need to take a microscopic look into our institutions to find out who our schools are working for, who they are not working for, what we can learn, and what we can celebrate.

In order to keep our canaries in the classroom and redefine, deconstruct, reconstruct, and revolutionize the mine, the proposed 10-Point Plan to transform the culture of our schools can be used as an organizing vehicle driven by a grounded theory of action. This chapter will outline a multipronged approach to facilitating change and promoting the possibility of collaborating with communities to implement the 10-Point Plan on a local level. The chapter will end with an immediate call to action for policy, practice, and research that focuses on what communities, K–12 schools, and universities can do right now to create more humane, relevant, and bold institutions to more equitably serve our students.

The PUEDES Approach: More Complexity and Relevance

The PUEDES approach described in Chapter 2 was developed from over 10 years of research directly in urban schools and communities serving primarily low-income Black and Latina/o youth. This approach suggests that stakeholders must be willing to step back from the "commonsense" explanations typically used to explain dropout and justify misguided or counterproductive educational policy. The PUEDES approach provides a much more nuanced, complex, and context-relevant analytical method of understanding why students are dropping out of school, while also providing a solutions-oriented guide to responding equitably and more accurately. Because the PUEDES approach encourages a look at factors associated with structure, culture, and individual agency, we not only are better informed about "why," but we can be better poised to act with community stakeholders. The PUEDES approach provides a 21st-century lens that facilitates rigorous understanding and advocacy for equity-driven action. However, before advocating for the 10-Point Plan, we need to critically understand what is going on, and the PUEDES approach helps us do just that.

Cross-Institutional Collaboration: Communities *and* Schools

Research has shown that the social, political, economic, historical, and cultural contexts of schools directly impact what happens in those schools (Noguera, 2003). That said, the ways in which we respond to the many challenges must include stakeholders that represent these different contexts and institutions. Not only have we found this to be a challenge in our work over the last 10 years, but in doing the work, we have framed our work in ways that give community stakeholders no other choice but to engage. We have also found a considerable number of unintentional consequences that have significantly benefited our efforts and our students' experiences and opportunities.

In order to implement the 10-Point Plan, schools cannot and should not do the work alone. Although many of the recommendations are centered on practices and policies that are directly shaped by actors in and around school systems, the 10-Point Plan is intended to be used as a leveraging point to provide bridges between the school and parents, business owners, school alumni, elected officials, and nonprofits. Like many of our students who typically lack the resources or information necessary to get to college, schools also need webs of support, particularly during financially difficult times. However, it must be noted that before, during, and after the global financial crisis, low-income children, and particularly students of color in the United States, have always attended public schools with strained resources and inequitable opportunities to learn. In other words, the inequality we see today is nothing new. However, our response can and should be new, novel, and bold.

Nevertheless, the community matters, and is filled with rich resources, even in communities that might be struggling economically and politically. There is a body of research suggesting that these communities have particular forms of cultural wealth (Yosso, 2005) and "funds of knowledge" (Moll, Amanti, Neff, & Gonzalez, 1992). The key is to create opportunities *through* the schools and *with* the community to capitalize on these powerful forms of wealth.

From my experiences with PROS in Boston, POWER in Miami, and PRAXIS in Southern California, university affiliation is a critical institutional asset that helps leverage resources, visibility, and credibility. In The PRAXIS Project, I applied for and received two modest, yet important, faculty start-up research grants intended for community-based research. These helped put the project on the university radar, and helped legitimize part of my work at the university. A university affiliation also helped leverage a handful of research assistants that helped with the overall research process. These university students also served as critical mentors to countless numbers of high school student-researchers. These research assistants were not only from the community, but were committed to serving their community.

Building a partnership between the university and the local schools facilitates opportunities for institutional agents to work directly with youth.

The PRAXIS Project also built several forms of political capital with various community partners. Our strategic relationship with the Martinez District Superintendent and school board facilitated access and stability with our project at Martinez High. Even when the situation grew tenuous as a result of our initial research presentation, our connection with the highest levels of leadership in the district not only legitimized our work and validated our presence, but these relationships also served as a source of encouragement when we thought that our time at the school might possibly come to an end. Finally, our access to the district leadership also facilitated our ability to influence key policy and practical changes occurring in the district. Because the Martinez superintendent was relatively new to the position, our work was timely, as he was committed and receptive to our recommendations.

One such recommendation stemmed from our research on student voice. We recommended that the district create spaces for student voice as a way to frequently check in on the culture of the school. With that recommendation, the superintendent instituted and facilitated monthly student forums at both of the district's high schools. He used the lessons learned and information from the students' voices to shape the way the district viewed the role of students in their own educational process. In fact, several concrete actions followed. For instance, a series of community partnerships were developed that engaged students in service activities related to community beautification and professional internships in local businesses. The district also adopted a theme of "connectedness" as a way to not only promote a culture of connecting students with adults, but also connecting community resources with the school, and therefore facilitating opportunities for students. The superintendent has repeatedly said publicly that our work spearheaded many ideas that are currently being instituted at the time of this writing.

Another layer of community engagement involved the active participation of local alumni, retired professionals, parents, community leaders, and elected officials. Many of these supporters were Chicana/o and/or Latina/o Martinez alumni who remained active and committed to progress in the community. Specifically, we have found that alumni from Martinez High were more than willing to give their time and energy to benefit the larger cause of The PRAXIS Project. They attended community engagement meetings, participated on subcommittees, and served as a powerful base of political support when advocating for changes in policies and procedures related to student engagement and dropout. For instance, after Year 1, a Martinez High alumni and head nurse at a local hospital opened up her home to The

PRAXIS Project, and invited alumni from her graduating class to hear about our work. This engagement led to an independent initiative between the Superintendent's Office and the promotion of health careers for all students at Martinez High and across the district.

In another situation, an alumnus, who was also a longtime community champion for education and local leader, became a strong supporter of The PRAXIS Project. He attended community-engagement meetings, encouraged other leaders to attend, and served on The Excellence Campaign Committee at Martinez High. This particular alumnus had not visited the school for quite some time, and after a few visits, was appalled at the poor physical conditions of the school. He observed trash on the floor, overflowing trash cans, graffiti, dilapidated buildings, peeled paint on walls, and the poor physical condition of the school's cafeteria. One particular and rather emotional moment occurred when this alumnus from the 1950s passed by one of the school's statues that was once a source of pride and ritual at Martinez. It was a waist-high, square structure built with brick and painted with Martinez High's school colors. On top of the structure was some kind of inscription that was dedicated by one of the school's graduating classes. The top of the structure had an indentation about 1 foot by 1 foot and about 3 inches deep. It was full of trash. As he was passing by, he stopped, and said, "this is unbelievable. This represents the pride of this school. We need to do something about this."

Shortly thereafter, this alumnus took it upon himself, aside from The PRAXIS Project, to organize a meeting with the superintendent, school principal, vice principal, and school board members, and proposed a school beautification effort. He sought to raise money to address some of the conditions in the school. Along with other alumni, he held fundraisers featuring prominent local politicians and community leaders. Rather than giving the money to the school, however, he created a fund to challenge groups of students to write a proposal for school beautification. "This will build school pride," he stated. While this was not a PRAXIS-driven initiative, it was triggered by the outreach PRAXIS spearheaded to give alumni an opportunity to engage with the school, help identify some of the challenges facing the school, and then do something about it.

In addition to alumni, parents became a powerful source of encouragement and support for The PRAXIS Project. While parent engagement was not one of our deliberate goals of the project, we certainly found refuge in the ways that parents emerged when we needed the support. When parents found out that we were committed to students' voices and experiences, they put their support behind us. One parent began to attend our research meetings, and served as a source of support for our project. She frequently stated, "we need to hear the students' voices." This particular parent told us that her daughter struggled to find her voice in high school, and felt that no one listened to students. As a senior in high school, this particular student was unsure about her plans, but decided to enroll in the local community college. About two years later, I received a message from the mother thanking us for the opportunity. She said that it was a turning point for her daughter, as it motivated her daughter to discipline herself to complete community college and pursue a degree in nursing.

The collaborative efforts emanating from The PRAXIS Project speak directly to the "public" nature of our public schools. Had the doors remained closed and had alumni and parents been kept out, none of the initiatives or opportunities would have been possible. Our work suggests that 21st-century community engagement requires that alumni, parents, and other key stakeholders have access to the on-the-ground conditions of schools, particularly those that are struggling to equitably serve their students. We have learned that our communities are on standby; they only need opportunities to engage. We viewed this as our role as university and/or alumni stakeholders in the community. The PRAXIS Project tackled the groundwork necessary to forge the partnership, the alumni jumped on board, and in the end, the students and the community benefited. Cross-institutional partnerships are vital for effectively responding to the dropout crisis facing our communities.

Sustainability

During The PRAXIS Project, our efforts at community engagement required a commitment to sustainability, and at the same time, illuminated the limits to our work. As in any situation, sustainability is beneficial when a particular result is sought. Sustainability is particularly important when trying to transform the conditions in complex institutions such as struggling schools that serve marginalized children and communities. Even though most educators and decision makers might know what is right, they often suffer from institutional amnesia, where people revert to the same-old, same-old practices and policies, particularly when the lid is lifted from any initiative that aims to intervene in, support, or improve current practice. This reality was particularly apparent during The PRAXIS Project's efforts in Southern California.

After spending two years exploring the strengths and the challenges at Martinez High School, we strategically pulled away from direct, on-the-ground research with youth, and decided to focus on dissemination and implementation of our findings at Martinez and across the region. We conducted various presentations at the local, regional, and national levels, and published our work in op-ed pieces, blogs, social media sites, and traditional academic outlets such as journal articles. We also delivered professional-development workshops for various schools and districts across the region and nationally. To maintain contact with the school, we launched and guided the school's Excellence Campaign™, as described in Chapter 4. The Excellence Campaign at Martinez sought to engage the school's stakeholders in a sustained dialogue and series of actions that would define, identify, celebrate, and learn from local "models of excellence" at the school and community levels. This work is driven by an Excellence Committee comprised of students, teachers, administrators, alumni, and other community stakeholders. The leader of these campaigns is intended to be a visible school leader, preferably the school principal, but not always. This person would need to be the champion behind the effort that helps mobilize support, ensure its sustainability, and see it through to completion during each Campaign.

As leaders of The PRAXIS Project, and as alumni of Martinez High, our team worked closely and collaboratively with the Excellence Committee at Martinez for one year. We helped launch two Excellence Campaigns, and provided technical assistance during the development of the process. In an effort to ensure its sustainability, the school leadership requested that students and teachers take ownership of the process of developing the campaign materials. The PRAXIS Project was all for this effort, as this was one of our goals—help build the school's capacity to lead efforts like the Excellence Campaign. During the third campaign, Martinez High enlisted the support of the school newspaper, the journalism class, its faculty representative, and members from a computer-design course to help construct the Excellence Campaign posters. While the process was not completely smooth, it certainly demonstrated the possibilities and sustainability of Excellence Campaigns when the school assumes responsibility, delegates responsibility to students and faculty, and eventually takes ownership of the Campaign.

This process of "letting go" was and continues to be difficult and speaks to our limits as a project. As much as we would like to drive the charge forward within the school, we remain school outsiders. Martinez, like most public schools, is on a strict schedule in which the time and physical location of students and teachers are always accounted for on any given hour/day. Our university schedules are much different, and served us well during our first two years, as we sought to understand the strengths and challenges within Martinez. In addition, we are simply unable to be there around the clock like the students, teachers, and administrators. Thus, it makes complete sense to have the school take ownership of the Campaign from within and The PRAXIS Project provide support when necessary. However, this does not excuse us from our responsibility, nor does it steer us away from our interest in promoting positive change within the school. On the contrary, we remain vigilant in our support and advocacy, but have to remain practical and realistic about our limitations in ensuring the sustainability of the effort. In order to facilitate change through the 10-Point Plan, the school must take ownership, as this process requires a strong, school-level champion to drive the charge forward.

Figure 5.1. Toward a 21st-Century Theory of Action

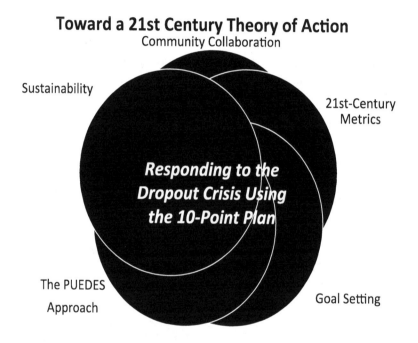

Proposing Bold, 21st-Century Metrics

There has been considerable debate about the appropriate metrics to use when it comes to measuring dropout. This book was not necessarily concerned about this particular debate, nor was it a goal of this book. My research suggests that the 10-Point Plan encourages us to reconsider the metrics we traditionally use to measure "effectiveness" or "success." Because these traditional metrics are outcome-oriented (i.e., test-score driven), they fail to capture the process-oriented nature of schooling. Lessons learned from PROS in Boston, POWER in Miami, and PRAXIS in the Inland Empire encourage us to consider these process-oriented influences that are vital to student engagement and success (see Figure 5.1).

For example, in early 2013, I was invited to join a select group of community leaders charged with creating a vision for the region through a strategic planning process. While education was an area of focus, so were health, economic development, housing, and other important issues. The two-hour meeting was particularly focused on a series of key education metrics that are typically found in most school systems—school readiness, literacy, promotion rates, reading and/or math scores, graduate rates, and the like. And while critically important, I found these metrics to be shortsighted and too simplistic for a 21st-century school system. Upon reflection from this meeting, I realized that we continue to recycle the same accountability measures mostly because our ways of understanding the dropout problem have been narrowly focused. In fact, the recent era of "Test Prep Pedagogy" triggered by No Child Left Behind only secured these narrow ways of understanding, and subsequently, responding. Rather than getting stuck in the same old metrics we are used to, I began to ask, "What are the conditions that are necessary for promoting school readiness," "on-target reading levels," and "high graduation and college-going rates?"

The lessons learned from all three projects in this book lead us to propose more bold and more process-oriented metrics that provide opportunities for teachers, counselors, school leaders, district officials, and school board members to understand and act, particularly in regions where a significant percentage of children live in poverty, and where there are concentrations or high percentages of children of color, English Learners, and immigrant students. In fact, years of empirical research in the field of education, and observations from my own research indicate that it is time to push toward metrics that capture the *processes* necessary for producing 100% proficiency in reading by third grade, middle school preparedness, and 100% high school graduation rates, for instance. If we are to envision a new community characterized by an equitable education system, civic responsibility and engagement, and a flourishing economy, we need to focus on metrics that shape the learning environments that are necessary to promote opportunity, learning, and academic achievement.

Accordingly, the 10-Point Plan outlined in Chapter 4 can be transformed into a series of concrete and measurable indicators that help us to understand how school processes contribute to student success. These metrics are framed as a "School Culture Index" (see Table 5.1), and can be used practically by school leaders, policy makers, and classroom teachers to assess their progress and reflect on educational practice. While these indicators are by no means comprehensive, we are likely to see significant progress, and provide our educators and schools with a blueprint of opportunity for our children, families, and communities. Until *we* frame what we measure, we will not make policy progress in ways that the 21st-century requires.

Table 5.1. Six 21st-Century Education Metrics—A School Culture Index

	Relation-ships	Student Voice	Recognition	Excellence	Marginalized Students	Community Engage-ment
Guiding Questions	Do all students have at least one meaningful relationship with a school adult?	In what ways are student voices used to guide school policy and practice?	How do educators recognize the existence of students in the school and/or community?	How are Excellence Campaigns™ used to strive for equity?	In what ways do schools actively learn from the voices and experiences of marginalized students?	How are community stakeholders (e.g., alumni) invited to participate to improve student engagement?
Metric	Internally produced by school.					
Who?	Assembled "Work Group" comprised of students, teachers, leadership, and community stakeholders.					
Timeline	1-, 3-, and 5-year timelines should be established by the "Work Group."					
Outcome	Improved levels of student engagement, graduation rates, and college-going rates.					

Goal Setting

When creating 21st-century metrics, we also need to engage in 21st-century goal-setting, particularly for low-income Black and Latina/o students in struggling schools with high dropout rates. While there are occasional "public" achievement targets such as those in the State of California assessment system (API scores), there are hardly any public targets that address graduation and/or dropout rates, frequency or quality of student-teacher relationships, or the ways in which schools engage students' voices to determine the quality of schooling students receive. Why do we excuse local systems of education from setting goals for their schools and communities around these particular themes? Part of the problem is related to the official metrics that are mandated from state and local policy measures mentioned earlier. This of course affirms why broadening the metrics to include 21st-century realities facing schools and communities is so vital.

Nevertheless, we need schools and districts to work collaboratively with community-based organizations, advocacy groups, alumni, parents, universities, businesses, the clergy, and other vital partners to establish concrete and realistic goals related to the 10-Point Plan. What kinds of student-teacher relationships should exist in our schools? What would student voice initiatives look like in our communities? What should we expect from an institution committed to excellence? Until we engage the 10-Point Plan in a useable way, we will struggle to facilitate buy-in and ownership over accountability. The days of using one test score to determine student promotion, academic level placement, or linguistic designation are over, and need to be replaced.

Broadening these 21st-century metrics and solidly identifying concrete 1-, 3-, 5-, and 10-year goals will require buy-in and monitoring from across the community. Districts and schools are already resource-strapped but can capitalize on the resources already available in the local community. Not only is this a smart use of resources, but it is an important way to ensure that schools and community stakeholders will work together and facilitate shared accountability.

However, such collaborative efforts should not be romanticized. We have learned from firsthand experience that there will always be the naysayers. There will always be the people who do not want to collaborate, even if it is in the best interest of our students and our communities. History, strained relationships, politics, and territorial feuds will be present. The challenge will be for key leaders to move beyond the "personal," and move the community toward a 21st-century reality that is opportunity-rich and dedicated to equity and social justice.

A Call to Action Now:
What We Can Do Today to Respond to the Dropout Crisis

There are three concrete steps schools, communities, districts, and policy makers can now take to move our schools forward and work toward building powerful cultures of student success. These three steps are intended to be driven by local leadership, and will require the buy-in and leadership to ensure implementation, appropriate monitoring systems, and accountability.

When it comes to action, it is important to share the good news. The good news is that we know what works. That is, there is no shortage of knowledge about what it takes to reduce dropout, increase graduation and college-going rates, and produce opportunity-rich schools that equitably serve all of our region's children and youth. The larger questions are, Are we bold enough to take on the challenge and create the conditions that transform daily practices in our schools? Are we bold enough to put relationships under the institutional microscope? Are we bold enough to create a vehicle to listen to and learn from students' voices? Below are three concrete actions to help us address these questions.

Policy action #1: Investing in relationships for student success.

Whereas the research shows that meaningful student-teacher connections, relationships, and interactions are significantly associated with students' social, emotional, and academic development, particularly in culturally and linguistically diverse communities, districts shall support schools in shaping learning environments that foster positive student-teacher relationships. To that end, districts should collaborate with schools to dialogue about, implement, monitor, and celebrate exemplary practices, programs, and policies that contribute to the development of healthy student-teacher relationships, particularly as they relate to student achievement and success.

Suggested Measurable Actions Include:

(1) School leadership shall initiate monthly dialogues (i.e., professional development) between students, teachers, staff, and community stakeholders about the definition and significance of student-teacher relationships in that particular school.

(2) School leadership shall assemble a school-based "work group" on the topic of student-teacher relationships, and devise relevant monitoring tools, specifically on student-teacher relationships.

(3) School leadership and faculty shall assess the degree to which the curriculum, pedagogical practices, and overall climate of learning reflects the school, community, and cultural context of the school as an opportunity, or missed opportunity to build student-teacher relationships.

(4) Work groups will devise a school-specific classroom-monitoring tool that provides constructive feedback to teachers on their engagement and interactions with students.

(5) District leadership and school boards will engage in monthly walk-throughs that focus on the relational climate of the school.

(6) Schools shall submit monthly updates on the progress and development of the relational culture that focus on positive (or negative) shifts in institutional culture.

(7) Work groups will devise a biannual, school-wide "Relationship Score Card" informed by data generated from the above efforts.

(8) Districts shall support schools in monitoring the impact of "Relationships Campaigns" (all of the above) on the overall culture of the

school, and their impact on the specific engagement and achievement of students, particularly African American and Latina/o youth.

Policy action #2:

Engaging students' voices to promote school connectedness.

Whereas the research shows that the inclusion of students' voices is significantly associated with student engagement, achievement, and success, particularly in culturally and linguistically diverse communities, the district shall support schools in shaping learning environments that actively engage students' voices. To that end, districts will collaborate with schools to dialogue about, implement, monitor, and celebrate exemplary practices, programs, and policies that contribute to the development of a school culture that values and utilizes students' voices to shape school- and district-level policy and practice, particularly as they relate to student achievement and success.

Suggested Measurable Actions Include:

(1) School leadership shall guide the implementation of monthly student-voice forums that capture the voices and experiences of all students. These should include high-, middle-, and low-achieving students.

(2) School leadership shall use the information generated from the forums to guide staff meetings and professional-development sessions to improve educational practice at the school and classroom levels.

(3) School leadership shall implement and monitor a diverse "work group" of students, teachers, staff, parents, and community stakeholders who measure the climate of students' voices and monitor its impact on student engagement and achievement over time.

(4) Schools shall ensure that historically marginalized students—disengaged students, those who act out, and those who are silent—are invited to participate. Such students might belong to particular school or community subcultures. Our research has demonstrated that these students are likely to provide profound, honest, and critical insight into the strengths and challenges of the school.

(5) School-based work groups should devise a school-specific classroom-monitoring tool that provides constructive feedback to teachers on their engagement with students' voices.

(6) District leadership and school boards will visit the monthly Student Voice Forums that focus on the climate of students' voices in schools.

(7) Schools shall submit biannual updates on the progress and development of the student-voice initiatives that focus on shifts in institutional culture.

(8) Work groups will devise a biannual, school-wide "Student Voice Score Card" informed by data generated from the above efforts.

(9) Districts shall support schools in monitoring the impact of "Student Voice Campaigns" (all of the above) on the overall culture of the school, and their impact on the specific engagement and achievement of students.

Policy action #3: Promoting a culture of excellence in every school.

Whereas our research in The PRAXIS Project shows that schools typically struggle with an explicit definition and commitment to excellence, districts shall support schools in initiatives that focus on creating a culture of excellence at each school. To that end, districts will collaborate with schools to dialogue about, implement, monitor, and celebrate exemplary practices, programs, and policies that contribute to the development of a school culture that values and utilizes excellence to shape school- and district-level policy and practice, particularly as they relate to student achievement and success.

Suggested Measurable Actions Include:

(1) Districts shall support school-based leadership to assemble and monitor an "Excellence Committee" comprised of students, teachers, administrators, staff, parents, alumni, and community stakeholders who guide "Excellence Campaigns" at each school.

(2) The Excellence Campaign shall define excellence, and school leadership shall guide dialogues with staff at staff meetings, at professional-development sessions, and with students.

(3) Excellence Campaigns shall identify "models of excellence" and celebrate these exemplars publicly. Ideas include posters, banners, newspapers, social-media outlets, district board meetings, local and regional businesses, government agencies, etc.

(4) Districts shall capitalize on the local talent by meaningfully engaging alumni in mentoring activities, scholarship development, and supporting the academic development of students.

(5) Districts shall support schools in monitoring the impact of "Excellence Campaigns" (all of the above) on the overall culture of the school, and their impact on the specific engagement and achievement of students.

Conclusion

In this book I made an attempt to transform the way we understand and respond to the dropout crisis facing our country, particularly for low-income Black and Latina/o students in the United States. Those of us who are committed to responding need to push our communities and institutions to move beyond simplistic and often deficit-oriented understandings and responses to the problem. If we continue to frame the problem as psychologically and behaviorally based, then we will continue to create solutions that just focus on behavior. If we continue to frame the problem as solely a matter of poverty, then we are likely to continue to blame people for their condition. If we continue to blame certain groups' cultural values, then we will never recognize the strengths that struggling people do bring to our schools and classrooms every day.

The PUEDES approach aims to respond to this crisis by pushing our understanding to one that is much more complex. The PUEDES approach makes us consider student (dis)engagement holistically, and provides theoretical and practical inroads that can be used to strengthen the ways teachers, counselors, parents, district officials, policy makers, community stakeholders, and even students understand and respond. The PUEDES approach also pushes us to realize that dropout is not the result of just poverty, culture, or individual will alone. The problem is much more complex, and requires us to be critical, compassionate, and relentless about finding solutions.

This book also walked us through three school- and community-based research initiatives across three regions of the United States—Boston, Miami, and the Inland Empire—that aimed to describe and discern some of the key challenges and possibilities in our schools and communities. The common denominator across the three regions was the concentration of poverty; the concentration of Black, Latina/o, English Learners, and immigrant students; and the pervasive drought of equitable educational opportunities in the public-school systems. These projects demonstrated that if you are poor, Black or Latina/o, an English Learner, and/or an immigrant student, it is highly unlikely that you will have a strong connection with an adult, have your voice heard, or be understood by the people who serve you on a daily basis. Yet, we also found situations where relationships were strong, students' voices were heard and engaged, and students were fully recognized. From these lessons learned, we presented a 10-Point Plan that focused on several critical elements that individually can facilitate more equitable opportunities for academic success in school, but collectively can transform the school-culture conditions that can work for all students, and produce engaged and successful students. It cannot be overstated—relationships, student voice, recognizing the entire existence of our students, leveraging the resources in the community—are among a handful of vital actions that schools and communities can collaborate on, policy makers can support, and researchers need to incorporate into research and measurement models and theoretical frameworks so that we move into the 21st-century with a consciousness of equity. Denying these elements only pushes us backward and contributes to inequity and injustice. Denying these elements also ensures that the next few decades of educational reform will completely miss the mark and leave us spinning into an abyss of perpetual failure, especially for children and communities that rely most on the public school system in the United States.

Lastly, I explored the seemingly common, yet elusive, reality that schools cannot do this work alone. Through a 21st-Century Theory of Action, we need cross-institutional efforts that engage vital community stakeholders, parents, alumni, and other key players, and they must work in tandem with school systems to create bold metrics that are relevant to that particular community, create concrete goals that are relevant to the 21st-century, and together assume responsibility for this lingering dropout problem facing our communities and country.

It is clear that the dropout and/or graduation-rate crisis is a concentrated reality; it disproportionately affects poor children and communities of color. Hence, it only makes sense that our practical and policy responses need to be just as deliberate and concentrated. When we dialogue about this looming challenge, let us recognize all of its ugliness and all of its promise. Let us be critical, and let us be constructive. Let us be democratic and inclusive, and let us be forthright in our pursuit of results. Let us be systematic, and let us be principled. Prioritizing school culture to confront the dropout crisis urges us to look inward for solutions, rather than outward for excuses. If schools and communities prioritize attention toward school culture, perhaps the dropout crisis can be a minor footnote in the nation's history, rather than an identifying marker of its ongoing struggle. To get there, we must collaborate, we must set goals, and we must be relentless in our pursuit of educational equity and excellence in our regional schools and communities for all of our students. We cannot fail another generation—economically, intellectually, morally, or politically—because of inequitable policies, practices, and framing of the issues. It is up to us. Our fortitude to act is our hope, and our hindrance. Let us dream of a new social, political, economic, and educational reality, and start the 21st-century with moral certitude, political conviction, and thoughtful action. Equity and excellence must be the goal for the schools, communities, and institutions that serve our children.

Bibliography

Ancess, J. (1998). Urban dreamcatchers: Planning and launching new small schools. In M. Fine & J. I. Somerville (Eds.), *Small schools, big imaginations: A creative look at urban public schools* (pp. 22–33). Chicago, IL: Cross City Campaign for Urban School Reform.

Anyon, J. (1980). Social class and the hidden curriculum of work. *Journal of Education, 162*(1), 67–92.

Ayala, J., Cammarota, J., Rivera, M., Rodriguez, L. F., Torre, M., & Berta-Avila, M. (in press). Red dawns of hope: An invitation to reconceptualize teacher education through PAR entremundos. A NLERAP (National Latino Education Research and Policy) document.

Balfanz, R., Herzog, L., & Mac Iver, D. J. (2007). Preventing student disengagement and keeping students on the graduation path in urban middle-grades schools: Early identification and effective interventions. *Educational Psychologist, 42*(4), 223–235.

Balfanz, R., & Legters, N. E. (2004). Locating the dropout crisis: Which high schools produce the nation's dropouts? In G. Orfield (Ed.), *Dropouts in America: Confronting the graduation rate crisis* (pp. 131–155). Cambridge, MA: Harvard Education Press.

Bartolome, L. (1994). Beyond the methods fetish: Toward a humanizing pedagogy. *Harvard Educational Review, 64*(2), 173–194.

———. (2002). Creating an equal playing field: Teachers as advocates, border crossers, and cultural brokers. In Z. F. Beykont (Ed.), *The power of culture: Teaching across language difference* (pp. 167–191). Cambridge, MA: Harvard Education.

Bridgeland, J. M., Dilulio, J. J., & Morison, K. B. (2006). *The silent epidemic: Perspectives of high school dropouts.* A report by Civic Enterprises in association with Peter D. Hart Research Associates for the Bill & Melinda Gates Foundation. Washington, DC: Civic Enterprises. Retrieved from http://www.saanys.org/uploads/content/TheSilentEpidemic-ExecSum.pdf

Brown, T. M., & Rodriguez, L. F. (2009). School and the co-construction of dropout. *International Journal of Qualitative Studies in Education, 22*(2), 221–242.

Cammarota, J., & Fine, M. (2008). *Revolutionizing education: Youth participatory action research in motion.* New York, NY: Routledge.

Cammarota, J. & Romero, A. F. (2009). A social justice epistemology and pedagogy for Latina/o students: Transforming public education with participatory action research. *New Directions for Youth Development, 123*, 53–65.

Cassidy, W., & Bates, A. (2005). "Drop-outs" and "push-outs": Finding hope at school that actualizes the ethic of care. *American Journal of Education, 112*(1), 66–102.

Center for Public Education. (2005). High-performing, high-poverty schools: Research review. Retrieved from http://www.centerforpubliceducation.org/Main-Menu/Organizing-a-school/High-performing-high-poverty-schools-At-a-glance-/High-performing-high-poverty-schools-Research-review.html

Children's Defense Fund. (2010, May 28). *State of America's children: 2010 report.* Retrieved from www.childrensdefense.org/child-research-data-publications/data/state-of-americas-children-2010-report.html

Conchas, G. Q. (2001). Structuring failure and success: Understanding the variability in Latino school engagement. *Harvard Educational Review, 71*(3), 475–504.

Conchas, G. Q. & Rodriguez, L. F. (2007). *Small schools and urban youth: Using the power of school culture to engage students.* Thousand Oaks, CA: Corwin Press.

Cordova, T. (2004). Plugging the brain drain: Bringing our education back home. In J. M. Mora & D. R. Diaz (Eds.), *Latino social policy: A participatory research model* (pp. 25–53). New York, NY: Haworth Press.

Creswell, C. W. (2012). *Qualitative inquiry and research design: Choosing among five approaches* (3rd ed.). Thousand Oaks, CA: Sage.

Datnow, A., Hubbard, L., & Mehan, H. (2002). *Extending educational reform: From one school to many.* London, UK: RoutledgeFalmer.

Datnow, A. & McHugh, B., Stringfield, S., & Hacker, D. (1998). Scaling up the core knowledge sequence: The implications of specifying content but not process. *Education and Urban Society, 30*(3), 409–432.

de los Reyes, E., & Gozemba, P. A. (2001). *Pockets of hope: How students and teachers change the world.* Westport, CT: Bergin & Garvey.

Duncan-Andrade, J., & Morrell, E. (2008). *The art of critical pedagogy: Possibilities for moving from theory to practice in urban schools.* New York, NY: Peter Lang.

Edmonds, R. (1979a). *A discussion of the literature and issues related to effective schooling.* St. Louis, MO: CEMREL.

———.(1979b). Effective schools for the urban poor. *Educational Leadership, 37,* 15–24. Retrieved from www.midwayisd.org/cms/lib/TX01000662/Centricity/Domain/8/2.EdmondsEffectiveSchoolsMovement.pdf

Edmonds, R. & Frederiksen, J. (1974). *Search for effective schools: The identification and analysis of city schools that are instructionally effective for poor children.* Boston, MA: Harvard University.

Elmore, R. F. (1995). Structural reform in educational practice. *Educational Researcher, 24*(9), 23–26.

Emerson, R. M., Fretz, R. I., & Shaw, L. L. (1995). *Writing ethnographic fieldnotes.* Chicago, IL: University of Chicago Press.

Ferguson, R. (2003). Teacher's perceptions and expectations and the Black-White test score gap. *Urban Education, 38*(4), 460–507.

Fine, M. (1987). Why urban adolescents drop into and out of public high school. In G. Natriello (Ed.), *School dropouts: Patterns and policies* (pp. 89–105). New York, NY: Teachers College Press.

———. (1991). *Framing dropouts: Notes on the politics of an urban public high school.* Albany, NY: State University of New York Press.

Fine, M. & Rosenberg, P. (1983). Dropping out of high school: The ideology of school and work. *Journal of Education, 165*(3), 257–272.

Foley, D., & Valenzuela, A. (2005). Critical ethnography: The politics of collaboration. In N. K. Denzin & Y. S. Lincoln (Eds.), *The SAGE handbook of qualitative research* (3rd ed., pp. 217–234). Thousand Oaks, CA: Sage.

Freire, P. (1973a). *Education for critical consciousness.* New York, NY: Seabury Press.

———. (1973b). *Pedagogy of the oppressed.* New York, NY: Seabury Press.

————. (1998). *The Paulo Freire reader* (A. Freire & D. Macedo, Eds.). New York, NY: Continuum.

Fry, R. & Lopez, M. H. (2012, August 20). Hispanic student enrollments reach new highs in 2011. Retrieved from http://www.pewhispanic.org/2012/08/20/hispanic-student-enrollments-reach-new-highs-in-2011/

Fry, R. & Taylor, P. (2012, August 1). The rise of residential segregation by income. Pew Research Center. Retrieved from http://www.pewsocialtrends.org/files/2012/08/Rise-of-Residential-Income-Segregation-2012.2.pdf

Gandara, P. C., & Contreras, F. (2009). *The Latino education crisis: The consequences of failed social policies.* Cambridge, MA: Harvard University Press.

Giddens, A. (1984). *The constitution of society: Outline of the theory of structuration.* Los Angeles, CA: University of California Press.

Graduate Summit Report. (2012). Building a Grad Nation report: Progress and challenge in ending the high school dropout epidemic. Retrieved from http://www.americaspromise.org/Our-Work/Grad-Nation/Building-a-Grad-Nation.aspx

Guinier, L., & Torres, G. (2002). *The miner's canary: Enlisting race, resisting power, transforming democracy.* Cambridge, MA: Harvard University Press.

hooks, b. (1994). *Teaching to transgress: Education as the practice of freedom.* New York, NY: Routledge.

Huber Perez, L. (2009). Disrupting apartheid of knowledge: Testimonio as methodology in Latina/o critical race research in education. *International Journal of Qualitative Studies in Education, 22*(6), 639–654.

Irizarry, J. (2011). Buscando la libertad: Latino youths in search of freedom in school. *Democracy and Education, 19*(1), Article 4. Retrieved from http://democracyeducationjournal.org/home/vol19/iss1/4

Kozol, J. (2005). *The shame of the nation: The restoration of apartheid schooling in America.* New York, NY: Crown Press.

Ladson-Billings, G. (2000). Racialized discourses and ethnic epistemologies. In, N. Denzin & Y. Lincoln (Eds.), *Handbook of qualitative research* (pp. 257–277). Thousand Oaks, CA: Sage.

Lauria, M., & Mirón, L. F. (2005). *Urban schools: The new social spaces of resistance.* New York, NY: Peter Lang.

Lipka, J. (1998). *Transforming the culture of schools: Yup'ik Eskimo examples.* Mahwah, NJ: Lawrence Erlbaum.

Lopez, N. (2003). *Hopeful girls, troubled boys: Race and gender disparity in urban education.* New York, NY: Routledge.

Maxwell, J. A. (1996). *Qualitative research design: An interactive approach.* Thousand Oaks, CA: Sage.

Maxwell, J. A. & Miller, B. (1991). *Categorization and contextualization as components of qualitative data analysis.* Unpublished manuscript.

Mehan, H., & Wood, H. (1975). *The reality of ethnomethodology.* New York, NY: John Wiley and Sons.

Meier, D., & Wood, G. (2004). *Many children left behind: How the No Child Left Behind Act is damaging our children and schools.* Boston, MA: Beacon Press.

Miles, M., & Huberman, M. (1994). *Qualitative data analysis*. London, UK: SAGE.

Moll, L. C., Amanti, C., Neff, D., & Gonzalez, N. (1992). Funds of knowledge for teaching using a qualitative approach to connect homes and classrooms. *Theory Into Practice, 31*(2), 132–141.

Nieto, S. (1999). *The light in their eyes: Creating multicultural learning communities*. New York, NY: Teachers College Press.

Noddings, N. (1992). *The challenge to care in schools: An alternative approach to education*. New York, NY: Teachers College Press.

Noguera, P. (2003). *City schools and the American dream: Reclaiming the promise of public education*. New York, NY: Teachers College Press.

Oakes, J., & Rogers, J. (2006). *Learning power: Organizing for education and justice*. New York, NY: Teachers College Press.

Orfield, G. (2004). Losing our future: Minority youth left out. In G. Orfield (Ed.), *Dropouts in America: Confronting the graduation rate crisis* (pp. 131–155). Cambridge, MA: Harvard Education Press.

Orfield, G., Losen, D., Wald, J., & Swanson, C. B. (2004). *Losing our future: How minority youth are being left behind by the graduation rate crisis*. Cambridge, MA: Civil Rights Project, Harvard University. Retrieved from http://civilrightsproject.ucla.edu/research/k-12-education/school-dropouts/losing-our-future-how-minority-youth-are-being-left-behind-by-the-graduation-rate-crisis

Payne, C. M. (2008). *So much reform, so little change: The persistence of failure in urban schools*. Cambridge, MA: Harvard Education Press.

Pianta, R. C., Stuhlman, M. W., & Hamre, B. K. (2002). How schools can do better: Fostering stronger connections between teachers and students. *New Directions for Youth Development, 93*, 91–107.

Rodriguez, L. F. (2003). Struggling to recognize their existence: Structure, power and relationships in three urban high schools. Unpublished Qualifying Paper, Harvard Graduate School of Education, Cambridge, MA.

———. (2005). Yo, Mister! An alternative urban high school offers lessons on respect. *Educational Leadership, 62*(7), 78–80.

———. (2008). "Teachers know you can do more": Manufacturing deliberate cultures of success for urban high school students. *Educational Policy, 22*(5), 758–780.

———. (2009). Challenging test prep pedagogy: Urban high school students educate pre-service teachers using liberatory pedagogy. *The Sophist's Bane, 5*(1–2), 30–36. Retrieved from http://equityandachievementseminars.wikispaces.com/file/view/Rodriguez+Challenging+Test+Prep+Pedagogy.pdf

———. (2010). What schools can do about the dropout crisis. *Leadership, 40*(1), 18–22.

———. (2011). Learning from the voices and experiences of students at Martinez High School: Towards a 10-point plan to reduce dropout, promote student engagement, and build 21st-century schools across the Inland Empire and beyond. The PRAXIS Project. Retrieved from http://www.praxisinschools.com

———. (2012). "Everybody grieves, but still nobody sees": Toward a praxis of recognition for Latina/o students in U.S. schools. *Teachers College Record, 114*(1), 1–31.

————. (2013). The PUEDES approach: Understanding and Responding to the Latina/o Dropout Crisis in the U.S. *The Journal of Critical Thought and Praxis, 2* (1), 122-152.

Rodriguez, L .F. & Brown T. M. (2009). From voice to agency: Guiding principles for participatory action research with youth. *New Directions for Youth Development, 123,* 19–34.

Rodriguez, L F. & Wasserberg, M. (2010). From the classroom to the country: Project POWER engages Miami's youth in action research initiatives for educational rights. *Journal of Urban Education: Focus on Enrichment, 7*(30), 103–107.

Rumberger, R. W. (2004). Why students drop out of school. In G. Orfield (Ed.), *Dropouts in America: Confronting the graduation rate crisis* (pp. 131–155). Cambridge, MA: Harvard Education Press.

————. (2012). *Dropping out: Why students drop out of high school and what can be done about it.* Cambridge, MA: Harvard University Press.

Rumberger, R. W. & Rodriguez, G. M. (2011). Chicano dropouts. In R. R. Valencia (Ed.), *Chicano school failure and success: Past, present, and future* (3rd ed., pp. 76–98). New York, NY: Routledge.

Sarason, S. (1972). *The culture of the school and the problem of change.* Boston, MA: Allyn & Bacon.

Shor, I. (1993). Education is politics: Paulo Freire's critical pedagogy. In P. McLaren & P. Leonard (Eds.), *Paulo Freire: A critical encounter* (pp. 25–35). London, UK: Routledge.

Solorzano, D. (1989). Teaching and social change: Reflections on a Freirean approach in a college classroom. *Teaching Sociology, 17*(2), 218–225.

Solorzano, D. & Yosso, T. J. (2001). From racial stereotyping and deficit discourse toward a critical race theory in teacher education. *Multicultural Education, 9*(1), 2–8.

Spatig-Amerikaner, A. (2012). Unequal education: Federal loophole enables lower spending on students of color. Center of American Progress. Retrieved from http://www.americanprogress.org/wp-content/uploads/2012/08/UnequalEduation.pdf

Stanton-Salazar, R. D. (2001). *Manufacturing hope and despair: The school and kin support networks of U.S.-Mexican youth.* New York, NY: Teachers College Press.

Strauss, A., & Corbin, J. (1998). *Basics of qualitative research: Techniques and procedures for developing grounded theory.* Thousand Oaks, CA: Sage.

Torre, M. E., & Ayala, J. (2009). Envisioning participatory action research entremundos. *Feminism & Psychology, 19*(3), 387–393.

Trueba, E. T. (1999). *Latinos unidos: From cultural diversity to the politics of solidarity.* Lanham, MD: Rowman & Littlefield.

U.S. Census Bureau. (2003). *Annual estimates of the population by sex and age of Hispanic or Latino origin for the United States: April 1, 2000 to July 1, 2003.* Retrieved from http://eire.census.gov/popest/data/national/tables/NC-EST2003-04-12.pdf (no longer accessible).

U.S. Department of Education. (2011). The condition of education 2011. Institute of Education Sciences, National Center for Education Statistics. Retrieved from http://nces.ed/gov/pubsearch/pubsinfo.asp?pubid=2011033

Valencia, R. R. (1997). *The evolution of deficit thinking: Educational thought and practice.* Washington, DC: Falmer Press.

————. (2011). *Chicano school failure and success.* New York, NY: RoutledgeFalmer.

Valencia, R. R. & Solorzano, D. (1997). Contemporary deficit thinking. In R. R. Valencia (Ed.), *The evolution of deficit thinking: Educational thought and practice* (pp. 160–210). Washington, DC: Falmer Press.

Valenzuela, A. (1999). *Subtractive schooling: U.S.-Mexican youth and the politics of caring.* Albany, NY: State University of New York Press.

Wehlage, G. G., & Rutter, R. A. (1986). Dropping out: How much do schools contribute to the problem? *Teachers College Record, 87*(3), 393–409.

Yang, K. W. (2009). Discipline or punish: Some suggestions for school policy and teacher practice. *Language Arts, 87*(1), 49–61.

Yosso, T. J. (2005). Whose culture has capital? A critical race theory discussion of community cultural wealth. *Race, Ethnicity, and Education, 8*(1), 69–91.

Index

Studies in the Postmodern Theory of Education

General Editor
Shirley R. Steinberg

Counterpoints publishes the most compelling and imaginative books being written in education today. Grounded on the theoretical advances in criticalism, feminism, and postmodernism in the last two decades of the twentieth century, Counterpoints engages the meaning of these innovations in various forms of educational expression. Committed to the proposition that theoretical literature should be accessible to a variety of audiences, the series insists that its authors avoid esoteric and jargonistic languages that transform educational scholarship into an elite discourse for the initiated. Scholarly work matters only to the degree it affects consciousness and practice at multiple sites. Counterpoints' editorial policy is based on these principles and the ability of scholars to break new ground, to open new conversations, to go where educators have never gone before.

For additional information about this series or for the submission of manuscripts, please contact:

Shirley R. Steinberg
c/o Peter Lang Publishing, Inc.
29 Broadway, 18th floor
New York, New York 10006

To order other books in this series, please contact our Customer Service Department:

(800) 770-LANG (within the U.S.)
(212) 647-7706 (outside the U.S.)
(212) 647-7707 FAX

Or browse online by series:
www.peterlang.com